# Scattering SEEDS of HOPE

*Also by Jeremy Marshall*

Beyond the Big C
Hope in the Face of Suffering
Meeting Jesus

*Also by Mary Davis*

Women of Faith
The Coming of the King (ed.)

JEREMY MARSHALL & MARY DAVIS

# Scattering SEEDS of HOPE

## EVANGELISM FOR THE DISCOURAGED AND INEFFECTIVE

10 Publishing
a division of 10 of those.com

British Library Cataloguing in Publication Data
A record for this book is available from the British Library

ISBN: 978-1-915705-51-8

Designed by Pete Barnsley (CreativeHoot.com)

Printed and bound in Great Britain by Clays Ltd, Elcograf S.p.A.

10Publishing, a division of 10ofthose.com
Unit C, Tomlinson Road, Leyland, PR25 2DY, England

Email: info@10ofthose.com
Website: www.10ofthose.com

1 3 5 7 10 8 6 4 2

# CONTENTS


Foreword ........ 1

Preface ........ 3

Introduction ........ 7

1. But I'm not an evangelist ........ 11
2. Scattering seeds ........ 21
3. The power of stories ........ 27
4. The power of questions ........ 39
5. The power of weakness ........ 51
6. The power of enthusiasm ........ 59
7. The power of social media ........ 67
8. The power of prayer and the Holy Spirit ........ 77

9. The power of God's Word .................................. 87

10. The miracle of salvation .................................. 97

My story and your story .................................. 101

Over to you .................................. 109

Resources .................................. 111

Endnotes .................................. 115

# FOREWORD

I knew Jeremy for many years. Nearly ten years ago he was diagnosed with incurable cancer and given months to live. God kindly gave him extra time and much of that he used to share his faith – both as a speaker at hundreds of events organised by churches up and down the country where he has talked about hope in the face of death, and one-on-one chatting with his friends and sharing the Bible. Facing death, he became gripped by the need to tell others. As the apostle John says, we must work while it's day because the night is coming, when no one can work.

I have to say that as I read this book I found myself punching the air. Why? First, because it underlines the *essentials* for evangelism: our heart-love for Jesus, belief that the Holy Spirit will do his miraculous work in our friends' lives, and a call to pray.

Secondly, this book *equips* me for evangelism. Jeremy passes on some brilliant questions, which I haven't used before, but which I'm already using, because they are simply the best questions to ask. I wish I'd known them years ago.

Thirdly, it *engages* with the culture as it is, confirming the fact that most people just don't have any idea about Jesus. So, we're in a new day and Jeremy's advice on the use of social media is so refreshing and motivating. I'm just so grateful for this book, written by someone who spent his life in the world of work and yet had such a good grip on the theology that needs to underpin authentic evangelism. The other great thing is that this book is short, so its lessons can be easily digested. I'm going to be handing it round my church and getting people together to talk about it.

**Rico Tice**

# PREFACE

Why should you read a book on effective evangelism when it's written by some City banker who has since gone to be with his Saviour?! It's a good question… but then this was no ordinary City banker. Jeremy was humbled, enthused, and empowered by his Lord in equal measure and in the most self-evident way. This was particularly true during Jeremy's last years that God gave him beyond the date the doctors had said it was a racing certainty that he would have died! In fact, on the sixth anniversary of his 'expected death day' we had a celebration lunch marvelling at, and utterly humbled by, what the Lord had done with this precious extra time.

It's current social practice to be driven by an urgent self-centred need to complete a bucket list before you die, as if this life is all that there is. However, that was not the instruction that Jeremy received from above when faced with the finality of his diagnosis. For him, there was a different path of intense usage and creative activity, entirely empowered by the Holy Spirit so actively at work in his life, using the 'train wreck' of a body that Jeremy became. The effort of writing this book came at a huge personal cost as the author persevered while under intense suffering.

Why a book on evangelism? Because at the heart of how Jeremy was used in those oh-so-precious final years was a wise and highly effective enthusiasm for telling anyone who would listen how hopeful, how real, how life-changing and enriching life with Christ can be. Jeremy was walking evidence of an intimate personal relationship with his living Saviour.

This man needed no 'religious crutch' despite being constantly irradiated by chemo and radiotherapy. He radiated the reality of God's Holy Spirit empowering him. The human 'suit' of his body was in tatters, but his soul, the real Jeremy Marshall, well, that was shining gloriously, made right for the eternity with His God that he knew he had already started to experience. Jeremy had certainty, and it filled him with a peace that no man can create, a peace that literally passes all human understanding.

Jeremy longed for others to know such assurance, not based in any way on his own righteousness, that, he said, was as shot to pieces as his physical body! He was desperately keen for all he came into contact with to have a living relationship with his Lord and Saviour.

In a world that shouts for individual rights, this book exudes the benefits of giving up such self-will. Each allotted day, Jeremy knew the loving peace and joy of walking with – or in his case, being carried by – a Saviour who has paid a price none of us can meet.

Jeremy Marshall echoed constantly the words Paul wrote in Philippians 1:

> *For to me, to live is Christ and to die is gain. If I am to go on living in the body, this will mean fruitful labour for me. Yet what shall I choose? I do not know! I am torn between the two: I desire to depart and be with Christ, which is better by far; but it is more necessary for you that I remain in the body. Convinced of this, I know that I will remain, and I will continue with all of you for your progress and joy in the faith, so that through my being with you again your boasting in Christ Jesus will abound on account of me (Philippians 1:21–26).*

That is why Jeremy has left you this book, written selflessly in his final months. Please read his book with an open heart, listening for God's calling, as Jeremy provides us with the most practical and exciting ways to share our faith. Don't put off for tomorrow what the Lord has called you to do today. This is an urgent call as those around us go through life knowing nothing of the eternal hope and grace on offer to them.

Let Jeremy share a thing or two about seeking out what the Lord will have each one of us do within our own unique circle of friends and contacts. May his practical advice make us all equally long for a similar relationship, imbued with the same passion, energy, enthusiasm and love for the lost who surround us all.

Enjoy – and please seek to put into practice, in God's strength, the fulfilling life of service that the author exemplified literally to the moment he went home.

**Richard Borgonon**

# INTRODUCTION

Most of the Christians I meet are discouraged when it comes to evangelism. They love Jesus and they'd love to be better at telling others how great he is. So what's the problem?

I think that many of us are afraid. We feel that society is very hostile and that everyone is against us. We think that people will be aggressive and unreceptive if we try to start a conversation about Christianity or Jesus. But, friends, this is simply not true: most people don't think about the church or the Christian faith from one month's end to the next.

In my experience, people are not generally hostile; they are indifferent. Empirical external research in the survey *Talking Jesus* backs up my claim.[1] It shows that most people have a Christian friend whom they like. The top traits in their Christian friends were that they were friendly (62%), caring (50%), good-humoured (33%) and generous (32%). The most negative traits were that 10% thought the practising Christian they knew was narrow-minded or naive and 9% said they felt they were hypocritical. So, yes, maybe there is a tiny minority of people who are hostile – but God may reach them too. Look at what happened to Saul of Tarsus![2]

Many people don't have the slightest clue about the Christian faith. They usually think it's about being good and doing their best. And lots of people know very little about the Bible. Some people know nothing at all. Zero! *Nada! Rien!* I can't tell you how many people have come up to me after I have spoken and say something like, 'Oh I didn't realise Jesus was a real person. I thought it was just a fairy story.' Or they'll say, 'That's a great story about Jesus. Did it really happen?' But by far the most common reaction I get is this: 'Why hasn't anyone told me about this before?' It's eerie how many times I have heard this. I hope you find this encouraging because it shows that God's Word has not lost its ancient power. People are often intrigued.

If you try reading a Gospel with a friend, you will find that the average person is really surprised by what they find in the Bible, even if they've had a good education. Usually, their understanding of what's in the Bible comes via Hollywood, or possibly from school assemblies. On the whole, it's not that our friends have considered Christ and rejected him – they simply don't know much about him. And they are rich soil for sowing the good seed of God's Word.

The world is in a mess right now. Ongoing worldwide challenges and crises at home have left people feeling worried about the future. Many are much more open to something new. Not necessarily Christianity, it can be anything – but there is a new openness.

But faced with this opportunity, many Christians are nervous and discouraged. Most of us are cowards and afraid of what people think of us. Isaiah 41:10 encourages us and promises us the presence of the Living God when we are afraid.

*So do not fear, for I am with you;*
*do not be dismayed, for I am your God.*
*I will strengthen you and help you;*
*I will uphold you with my righteous right hand.*

I love Jesus and you love Jesus – but we're not always very good at explaining that to our friends and family. Sometimes it's a relief to admit this. Many of us feel guilty. But feeling guilty is utterly counterproductive. Others don't say very much for fear of getting it wrong. What we all need is help and encouragement. I want to encourage you and hopefully equip you to share the fantastic news of the gospel. It is uniquely wonderful news – and news that our friends and family desperately need to hear.

**Jeremy Marshall**

Last year, I came across a Facebook post on evangelism where Jeremy shared three questions that he loves asking people. Later that morning, and thanks to those three questions, I had the best conversation about the Lord and the gospel that I'd had in ages as I chatted to the plumber who was mending my kitchen tap. I reached out to Jeremy on Facebook and offered to help him put his insights into a book. To my delight, he responded with characteristic enthusiasm just a few hours later. I'm thanking God for Jeremy and praying that many of us will be encouraged by his bold yet gentle wisdom which I've found to be so respectful and liberating.

**Mary Davis**

1

# BUT I'M NOT AN EVANGELIST

Can you ride a bike? Or maybe drive a car? How did you start? Probably very slowly in an empty car park, with great fear and trepidation. Certainly not in the fast lane of the motorway. Learning to drive takes a lot of practice. We need plenty of encouragement along the way. But slowly, slowly, you keep improving until, after many years, it feels entirely natural. Sharing our faith is much the same.

## EASY AS PIE

Some people say that evangelism is easy. They say that you just need three things: you need to understand and believe the gospel, you need the Holy Spirit and you need somebody to tell. All Christians by definition have the first two – and unless you are on a desert island, you also have the third. Simples! No problem. No training needed.

Off you go. Go and evangelise the world. It's easy – like falling off a log.

But it's not easy, is it? I think that evangelism is almost uniquely difficult and we need all the help we can get. How can we tell it's so difficult? Because not many of us do it! How many of the highly trained graduates leaving Bible college in the UK go on to be evangelists? Almost none. How many of them go on to be Bible teachers or church workers? Almost all. And once they're pastors, how much of their time do they spend in personal evangelism? Relatively little.

Why? Precisely because it's so hard to evangelise! It's much easier for pastors to sit in their studies consulting commentaries and producing finely crafted sermons for their congregations (an important task) than going out to find uninterested non-Christians to talk to. It's easier to attend conferences discussing how to unpack the Bible than to look at a Bible passage with non-Christians who aren't at all convinced. And the organisational demands on church leaders are greater than ever before which makes it hard to prioritise evangelism.

What about the rest of us? We don't find evangelism very easy either. What makes it hard? Fear mainly. The fear that I can't do it. The fear of a negative reaction from our friends. The feeling that nobody is that interested anyway. The thought that there's no point in getting into a hostile conversation or risking a friendship for no reason. The worry that we might jeopardise the relationship by saying too much. For all those reasons, we can't find it in us to cross what evangelist Rico Tice calls 'the painline'.[3]

## TAKE HEART

Training in the local church is, I believe, the best way to overcome fear. I'm not talking ivory towers and 16-week evangelism courses and I'm certainly not talking head knowledge. I'm thinking about teaching a child to ride a bike – a hand in the small of their back, encouraging them along.

Take heart from the disciples. They were truly terrible evangelists and pretty much everything they touched in this area turned to disaster. They turned away children who wanted to come to Christ. They wanted to unleash destruction on people who didn't accept them. They were fearful and lacking in faith time after time. When the soldiers came for Jesus in the garden of Gethsemane, they ran away in blind panic. They constantly missed the point of what Jesus was saying. They argued about which of them was the greatest.[4]

And what was Jesus' reaction to their (and our) ineptitude and incompetence in evangelism and discipleship? Incredible patience and incredible training! Jesus models, encourages, teaches, rebukes and coaches them in evangelism. This is why they were 'good to go' in Acts – plus, of course, they were now armed with the power of the Holy Spirit. As J M Boice points out, every time we read in Acts about someone being filled with the

Holy Spirit, the next thing that happens is that they teach others about Christ.[5]

## A WORD TO THE PASTORS

Pastors, are you modelling evangelism to your church family? That's how the Lord led his disciples.[6] Are you helping your congregation overcome their enormous fears about evangelism by doing it yourself? Otherwise, there's a danger of being like generals in the First World War safely behind the lines in their chateaux, sending the poor old privates 'over the top'. Those of us who are pastors should be coaching, encouraging, supporting, helping, advising and mentoring those we serve and modelling how to share our faith. The local church is the lifeboat to reach the drowning world and the volunteer crew needs to be trained. Otherwise, they will remain safely but ineffectively tucked up in the harbour!

Dear leaders, do what you can. It's hard because many leaders are busy, tired and discouraged. Is there someone nearby who you could meet for a coffee and find out what they think about faith and the gospel? Could you find one friend and, after a while, invite them to look at a passage of the Bible with you? Might someone you know come to an event that your church is holding? Even if they decline (as they may well do!), you have started to be a model to your congregation. Tell your church about your failures. When we teach our children or a friend to drive and they keep stalling, we don't say, 'Why did you do that? I never stalled when I was learning.' More likely, we'll say, 'You should have seen my mum teaching me to drive. It was like a mad kangaroo had got into the engine!' Leaders can encourage their flocks by sharing their stories of personal evangelism – and especially their failures!

## A WORD TO THE CHURCH FAMILY

Just in case you thought that evangelism was just for pastors, take a look at the Bible and the early church.

Pastor Jonathan Griffiths points out in *Preaching in the New Testament* that 'the New Testament expects all Christians to engage in word-based evangelism.'[7] In other words, in the New Testament, it's clear that we should all be talking to others about the good news of Jesus Christ. Preaching in church is a particular activity to which not everyone is called, but there are many other words in the New Testament about evangelism such as 'announce', 'teach', 'admonish', etc. – and we can all be involved in that. Jonathan Griffiths talks about the interplay between the word ministry of Christians in general and the word ministry that church leaders do. We, the congregation, receive instruction from our pastors and learn about the Bible, then we pass it on to our friends in an easily accessible format. And we have opportunities and credibility with our friends that the pastor doesn't have and, of course, our conversations with them allow for questions in a way that a sermon doesn't.

This was what happened in the days of the early church. As Michael Green says in his excellent book, *Evangelism in the Early Church*, 'Communicating the faith was not regarded as the preserve of the very zealous or of the officially designated evangelist ... The ordinary people of the church saw it as their job: Christianity was supremely a lay movement, spread by lay missionaries.'[8]

So don't think that you need to wait until you've got a formal qualification in theology or evangelism. That's not the kind of training I'm talking about. Evangelism is something we learn by practice. That's what we do when we do sport, of course. We learn as we play. We don't just study the theory of football, we *play* football – and as we play, we are trained by the coach and we get better at it. Nobody says you have to study the theory of football before you play it – we just get on and play, and learn as we go along.

But, equally, nobody says you don't need any training. We learn by kicking the ball – and being told how to kick it better and further and more accurately. Most training is like that – it's continuing and continuous encouragement, advice, mentoring and coaching. It's giving it a go. Hopefully, this book will be a part of that training.

Evangelism is also a team sport – and the team should be, above all, our local church but also the whole Christian community. As far as I can recall, every person I've introduced to Jesus has had some kind of prior Christian interaction. Someone else has often started off a conversation about the gospel and then I've found that I'm the one to take it on another stage.

Why do we need training and encouragement in evangelism? Because, along with prayer, it's the hardest thing in the Christian life. Only with God's help, the power of the Holy Spirit and useful training, in the sense I've described, will we get better at talking about Jesus Christ.

## A PERSONAL WORD

God has put us all in different circumstances – with a unique circle of friends and contacts. We all have different backgrounds and a different story to tell. We all have advantages. I am very aware that I have been given many.

I have a very big circle of friends and I love talking – perhaps more than listening?! I grew up in a strongly Christian home where the Bible was poured into us morning, noon and night. Each Sunday, I would have at least three hours of Bible-based teaching from my father who was the pastor. At the time, I hated it and found it exceptionally boring – as I told my father! But it means I have a very deep knowledge of the Bible. At university, I studied History and when people started asking me about the ancient world in which the Gospels are set, it was right up my street. I was CEO of a bank. I'm 6 ft 2.

And I have incurable cancer. Yes, that is a big advantage – though a very painful one, admittedly. But it is an advantage because it makes people compassionate and sympathetic to my predicament and often intrigued by my story.

Now you are not me but, if you think about it, we all have something that God has given us which can be helpful. We also all have a unique circle of friends, colleagues and acquaintances – those we rub shoulders with regularly who we might begin to reach.

One word of warning. The advice in this book comes from my experience of how to talk to friends in an easy and relaxed way. And yet, despite all my advantages, I sometimes talk to someone who reacts very negatively and gives me a 'right hook'. There is an innate offence to the gospel and, however skilfully we talk about Jesus and the gospel, sooner or later someone will attack us, usually verbally. When that happens, please remember that our identity is in Christ. What matters is what the Lord thinks of us – not other people's opinions. He warns us to expect hostility and he promises to be with us and help us when that happens.

At the end of each chapter, I have included a couple of things to help you think and pray about how you can share the gospel with the many, many people around us who do not know the wonderful love of Jesus for themselves.

## THINK IT THROUGH

- Pastors, Paul writes to the church at Philippi, 'Whatever you have learned or received or heard from me, or seen in me – put it into practice. And the God of peace will be with you' (Philippians 4:9). How can we intentionally give our flock a good example of what it is to share our faith with those who don't yet know Jesus?

- I have shared the advantages and opportunities that my circumstances have given me but all of us have advantages and opportunities. Why not take a few minutes to make a list of your own?

# 2

# SCATTERING SEEDS

Did you ever grow cress seeds when you were little? Or perhaps you've scattered some grass seed in an attempt to patch up a hole in the lawn? Or maybe you're a full-on expert who knows their *Tropaeolum majus* from their *Helianthus annuus*. When my younger son was small, he scraped a hole in the ground with a spoon and planted some poppies which are still flourishing many years later!

Seeds are tiny. They're unthreatening. But, given time, they grow and produce a great crop.

## SCATTERING SEEDS OF HOPE

Think about the farmer in Mark 4. Let's imagine the scene. It's early, the sun is just coming up and the farmer grabs his seed bag. He puts its long strap over his shoulder and heads out to the field. There's a patch behind the old barn that needs resowing. He smiles to himself as he walks – the weather is perfect today and it shouldn't be a long job. He reaches into the old leather bag and scoops out a handful of seed, rubbing them carefully between his fingers, feeling their rough texture. He leans forward slightly and, with a practised hand, begins to sow, scattering the seeds across the ground in an even pattern, making sure to cover every inch of the soil. The tiny grains fall lightly onto the bare soil.

Try and imagine it. The seeds are so small. Some of them will take; some of them won't. The whole process of sowing is gentle and quiet, unspectacular and easily missed. The farmer simply tosses out the seeds onto the earth – that's all he can do. He can't *make* the seeds grow – it will take rain and sun, good soil and the grace of God. The farmer knows that if he sows the seed, the crops will grow. He has to be patient.

Take a moment to read the passage from Mark's Gospel.

> *Listen! A farmer went out to sow his seed. As he was scattering the seed, some fell along the path, and the birds came and ate it up. Some fell on rocky places, where it did not have much soil. It sprang up quickly, because the soil was shallow. But when the sun came up, the plants were scorched, and they withered because they had no root. Other seed fell among thorns, which grew up and choked the plants, so that they did not bear grain. Still other seed fell on good soil. It came up, grew and produced a crop, some multiplying thirty, some sixty, some a hundred times (Mark 4:3–8).*

Have that picture of the farmer in your mind as we think about evangelism. Your job and my job is to throw out a few seeds and see what happens. Will they grow? Or will they land on the path and get eaten by the birds? That's not up to us. It's up to God. Our business is to scatter the seed as best we can and see what happens. We just have to take that first step. The Word of God is inherently tremendously powerful. But seed is no good if it stays in the bag. It needs to be sown. Friends, let's sow!

## SMALL BUT POWERFUL

How do we sow? At work, a colleague might ask, 'How was your weekend?' I might say something like, 'I had a lovely weekend, thanks. Our church had a great barbecue.' Some people will change the subject but other people will ask you more. Changing the subject is fine. Asking more is fine. You've flagged up that you go to church. Just leave it at that and see how people react. It's about sowing seeds. No one in my office was ever offended by conversations like that.

Here's another. A friend says, 'The world is so depressing right now.' I nod my head, 'Yes, I absolutely agree. It is. But I find my church – or my faith, or, best of all, Jesus Christ – so helpful.' Again, pause to assess their reaction. Some people are interested in exploring this further, others are not. Just scatter some gospel seeds. More than we think will land on good soil.

Or perhaps we could think about it in terms of knocking on a door. We're trying a door and seeing what happens. We may be surprised to find which ones open when we knock gently. We can't unlock the door. We don't even know which doors have been unlocked by the Holy Spirit. Our job is simply to knock gently and see if the door is opened.

Everyone's situation is different and we need to adjust our approach to our own context and our own friends. We are simply scattering the seed. Whether it lands on good soil or a concrete path is wholly up to God. Some seed will land on soil that is freshly dug and ready for planting. But often the seed will land on a rocky footpath, or the birds will come and eat it up, or the thorns will stop it growing. That's God's business, not ours. Ours is simply distributing the seed. It just needs to be scattered – indiscriminately, as often as possible, and in as large handfuls as we can manage.

Maybe there's a neighbour you smile at as you put the bins out. A parent at the school gate. Someone who's always at the same bus stop. Or maybe you work in a busy office or hospital, or on a rota with a different group of people each shift. Perhaps we can only manage a passing comment or a brief chat over a cup of coffee. That's OK. We do what we can, where we can. God has made us his ambassadors. Every chance we have, we can promote our 'home country'. We can simply throw out a topic and see who picks up on it, keeping it low key and open. Someone may pick up on the conversation at some point – and if they don't, that's down to God.

Seed is incredibly small. Maybe the only thing we have time to say is, 'That's why I find Jesus amazing.' It may be small – but it's unbelievably effective and powerful. I've had so many people react to my comments like that by then asking me the question I long to be asked, which is, 'Why do you like Jesus so much?'

Finally, and most importantly, we are completely reliant on the Holy Spirit. The Holy Spirit unlocks the doors of people's lives from the inside – but we can't tell which people he's working in! Time and time again, it's the people I think are very unlikely to be interested in God who turn out to be most interested. I often discover later that something happened to them – maybe someone else spoke to them years ago or they went to an event I knew nothing about or a particular situation in their past keeps nudging them to think about God.

For example, a friend of mine from a Hindu background wanted to ask some questions about Hinduism and Christianity, so I talked to a Christian friend who had also grown up as a Hindu. I always keep a friend's identity and what they've said to me confidential, but when I described the person to my Christian friend, he said, 'It's not X, is it?' I laughed and said, 'Yes, it is.' It turned out the two of them had chatted about the Christian faith many years before. When I asked my original friend about the event, he said it was that discussion that had started him on the road to considering Christianity. I had not the slightest notion. In fact, I didn't even know they had ever met.

The Holy Spirit is at work behind the scenes in our friends' lives. God's Word is powerful and, once sown, it keeps on working. So, we don't need to feel guilty or inadequate. We simply need to take the opportunity to speak about Christ and to scatter gospel seeds wherever and whenever we can, praying that the Holy Spirit would be at work.

## THINK IT THROUGH

- I might say something like, 'We had a great barbecue at church on Sunday' or 'That's why I find Jesus amazing.' Think through some words or phrases that would be natural to you, that you could intentionally use to sow seeds of hope in someone's life.
- What are you doing this coming week? Might there be a chance to say something about your gospel hope? What might it be?

3

# THE POWER OF STORIES

There's a story about Jesus that I particularly love.

One day, Jesus said to his disciples, 'Let's go to the other side of the lake.' So, they all got into the boat and Jesus went to sleep. In the middle of the lake, a terrible storm broke out. The disciples were experienced sailors and they knew the lake very well but this storm was different. The boat began to sink. But Jesus stayed asleep through it all, lying in the middle of the boat with his head on a pillow.

Frustrated, the disciples roughly shook Jesus awake. 'We're drowning!' they said. 'Don't you care?!' Jesus got up and, with one word, he calmed the storm. Suddenly, the winds dropped and the waves ceased. It went from a raging storm to a millpond. That shows something supernatural had happened because usually, even when the wind drops, the waves take a while to subside. Then something very curious happened. The disciples were even more afraid!

They were more terrified in the still of the millpond than they had been in the raging storm. Why? Because Jesus' identity began to dawn on them. This ordinary man who was tired and fast asleep was also God, because only God can calm a storm like that.

Do you find that when someone tells a story, you relax just a bit? We all love stories. They're engaging and unintimidating. They're personal and intriguing.

## HERE'S ANOTHER STORY

A while ago I was giving an evangelistic talk to some City workers during their lunch break. There was a Q&A afterwards and someone objected to what I'd said.

'Are you really saying, Jeremy, that if there were two people in the City, one was a scoundrel and a crook and wasted all his money on drugs and prostitutes, but came to faith at the end of their life, they would be accepted by God? But if there was someone else who had lived a very moral life and given lots of money to charity, but felt no need of God, they wouldn't be forgiven? It doesn't make any sense.'

It was a good, open and honest question. I wonder how you would have answered it. This is what I said: 'It's funny you should ask me that because people asked Jesus the very same question, and this is what he said…' And I told him – as you also would be able to do – the story of the Prodigal son and his brother.[9] It went something like this…

Jesus told a story about a man who had two sons. One day, the younger one came to him and said, 'Dad, I want my inheritance now.' He was basically saying, 'I wish you were dead, Dad.' The father gave him his share and the young man went off and lived the high life. Soon, there was a terrible economic crash and he ran out of money. To survive, he had to take care of pigs which was the ultimate humiliation for a good Jewish boy. One day, he thought to himself, 'This is crazy! I'd be better off as one of my dad's servants.' And he set off.

His father had never given up on his son coming home. And that morning, he couldn't believe his eyes. There was his boy in the distance. The old man did something very undignified. He hitched up his robes, ran as fast as he could and threw his arms around the boy, pig muck and all. He brushed aside his son's apology and said, 'We must have a party!'

Soon the man's older son came in from the fields and asked what all the noise was. When he heard about his brother, he was really angry and refused to come in. He said to his father, 'I've been slaving away for you for years and you never even gave me a party. But this reckless son of yours comes home and you go crazy!' The father turned to him and said, 'Everything I have is yours, son. But shouldn't we celebrate? We thought your brother was dead – but he's alive.'

And that's where it ends. As we hear the story, we're supposed to understand that the father is God – and we are either like the younger brother or the older brother. The younger one realises that God loves him and owes him nothing, and he decides to rely on the father's love.

The older one thinks his father owes him a favour because he's been good – and he doesn't realise how much he loves him. And Jesus is saying that we need to be like the younger brother and come home. We do this by believing in Jesus' promise that he offers us a way home to the Father through his death on the cross.

At the end, I added, 'Perhaps if Jesus had told the story today, he would have described the two brothers as City workers!'

The person asking the question was surprised by the story of the Prodigal son. He had never heard it before – he didn't even know it was in the Bible.

## WHY STORIES?

What's so helpful about using stories? Well, first, it's a model drawn straight from Jesus himself. He was the greatest theological teacher of all time. And the majority of his teaching was in the form of stories often called parables. 'With many similar parables Jesus spoke the word to them, as much as they could understand.'[10]

Stories are also memorable and easy to understand. They fit really well into our culture which, rightly or wrongly, values stories and personal contributions above abstract propositions. Stories are useful in dealing with tricky questions. For each question that someone asks me, I always try to respond by telling a Gospel story.

For example, someone might ask, 'What about other faiths?' I usually tell them about John 4, and the Samaritan woman. I tell them about the tender way in which Jesus breaks down the religious barriers (as well as the other barriers between them) and explains to her what true worship looks like.

When asked, as I often am, about the hypocrisy of Christians and our sex-obsessed world, I turn to John 8 and talk about the actions of Jesus with the woman caught in adultery. Without condoning her sinful living, he challenges the hypocrisy of those around her. At the same time, he calls her to be the recipient of his grace, mercy and forgiveness. Have a look at the passage (in particular John 8:7) and see the remarkable way that Jesus shines a light on how hypocritical the woman's critics were.

When someone says, 'Well, I'm not religious,' I laugh and go straight for John 3. I can have such an enjoyable time telling them the story of Nicodemus. I explain how Nicodemus was a religious person – rather like the older brother in the story of the Prodigal son. But Jesus says to him, 'You must be born again.' Nicodemus couldn't have been more religious – but Jesus says that isn't the point at all! It's not about being religious.

Or I might talk again about the woman Jesus meets in the very next chapter. She was a sexually immoral woman who is rather like the younger brother. She's a Samaritan and has clearly got some kind of religious background but it seems like that was in the distant past – it appears she's now living a sexually immoral life and would be the last person who would be interested in Jesus Christ. But she has a great discussion with Jesus about worship and religion and life. In the end, she is so taken by him and what he has to say that she races back to her village to persuade all her friends and neighbours to come and meet him.

I often get the comment, 'I can't believe in a loving God with so much suffering.' Suffering is such a huge topic. Sometimes people bring the question of suffering up thinking that it's a knock-down argument against the existence of a loving God – but, of course, some people talk about suffering because they are grieving a deep, personal loss. You'll have to think what will work in your circumstances and with your friends but let me tell you what I might say and then you can adapt it. I love to tell people the story of Jesus and the widow of Nain in Luke 7. When Jesus saw that this woman had lost her only son, having previously lost her husband, we're told that, 'His heart went out to her and he said, "Don't cry."' Jesus was deeply compassionate and kind in the face of suffering. And I have experienced that compassion and kindness over and over again. He is not a distant God; he is with us in our suffering.

Another episode in the Gospels which speaks about suffering is Jesus' deep grief over the death of Lazarus in John 11. We see how Jesus experienced sadness and suffering himself, and how he wept when his dear friend Lazarus died (John 11:35). We see how Jesus didn't stay in the glory of heaven – how he came and lived on the earth as one of us and experienced the pain and suffering that we all encounter as human beings living in a fallen world. Later in that chapter, we see that Jesus not only *cares* about human suffering, he is also *powerful* to do something about it. Even though Lazarus had been dead for four days, Jesus demonstrated his power over death and evil by bringing Lazarus back to life. That doesn't mean, of course, that he will always heal us, or take away our suffering – but it does mean that he's there with us when we are going through dark times.

What about when someone asks a question about their doubts and fears? I love to tell them the story of Jesus in the boat, in the middle of the storm, with his disciples (Mark 4). I might also talk about the loving and gracious way he deals with Thomas' doubts in John 20. (Although maybe he should be called Honest Thomas, rather than Doubting Thomas.) I might tell them of a recent experience of Jesus being in the boat with me in the middle of a storm I have been going through.

Once you know a Bible story well, you can use it almost word for word. I find that certain phrases jump out for me: 'But while he was still a long way off' (Prodigal son), 'Were not our hearts burning within us?' (Road to Emmaus), 'Jesus wept' (Lazarus), 'Don't you care if we drown?' (Jesus in the storm), 'Father, if you are willing, take this cup from me; yet not my will, but yours be done' (Mount of Olives).[11]

Often, of course, a friend asks an unexpected question and I find that it's in those moments that the Holy Spirit prompts us with the right words to say. Recently, for example, someone said to me, 'My husband just died. He didn't have any belief. Where is he now?' I thought, 'How on earth do I answer that? I must be truthful but also compassionate.' And then suddenly the story of the thief on the cross flashed into my mind, and I talked about the grace shown to this poor man by Jesus as he was dying and about how Jesus is the only one who is able to judge the heart of any person.

## THE POWER OF THE SEED

Another reason for using stories – and an important one – is that the Word of God itself is incredibly powerful. God's Word is much more powerful than anything we can say from our own intellect and our own creativity. 'For the Word of God is alive and active. Sharper than any double-edged sword.'[12]

It's so important for us to use the Word of God in our evangelism and talk about it naturally, in ways that people can really understand. I'm not talking about stopping a conversation and suddenly pulling out our large, black, leather-bound Bible and reading a passage to someone or sending them a link to a sermon. Those things can run the danger of being unnatural and impersonal. It can break the natural flow of our discussion and risk our friend's feelings. There's a danger that our friend might feel we are 'Bible-bashing' them, as people sometimes say.

Instead, if we naturally, simply tell a Bible story or a verse in our own words, it retains their interest. It continues the conversation and often leaves the opportunity to take things further. I've been amazed at the way in which after doing this a few times, retelling the story comes really naturally. It's relatively simple to do and is also good for our own hearts and Christian growth as well.

As we acknowledge that it's God's Word that has the power, not our own, we are enabled to respond by saying something like, 'Oh, that's a great question. You know, it reminds me of a Bible story, which I found so interesting ...' and off we go.

Short and snappy is the best. Tell the story naturally and briefly. In our ever-increasingly biblically illiterate world, almost nobody knows any of the Bible stories. If they respond positively, we could offer to look at another Bible passage with them. You will find, I guarantee, that most people are gripped by the stories. 'Does Jesus raise Lazarus from the dead?' asked a friend I was reading the Bible with, eagerly. 'Yes,' I replied, 'he does – just wait a few minutes!'

This way, our friends can come to meet the hero of the Bible and the hero of God's plan through the work of the Holy Spirit. He often works with immediacy and power and draws them into wanting to know more. It's as if telling people Bible stories acts as a trailer for the main film of the gospel message.

## MAKING MUCH OF JESUS

A third reason for using stories and examples from the Bible, particularly in answering people's questions, is that we want to make much of Jesus.

'And beginning with Moses and all the prophets, he explained to them what was said in all the Scriptures concerning himself.'[13] The whole Bible is about Christ. If we use the Bible to answer our friends' questions, in our own words, we will keep the flow of conversation pointing towards Christ. Telling stories about the Lord from the Gospels of Matthew, Mark, Luke and John brings him into the conversation in such a natural way.

Charles Spurgeon was a great preacher of a bygone age. He used to tell a story that if you were lost, every village and every hamlet in England would have a road to London. And if you found the road to London, you'd find where you should be going.[14] In his illustration, he would say that speaking about Jesus is like keeping on the London road.

> *Do you not know that from every little town and village and tiny hamlet in England there is a road leading to London? Whenever I get hold of a [Bible] text, I say to myself, 'There is a road from here to Jesus Christ, and I mean to keep on His track till I get to Him.'*

Even when Spurgeon was preaching from a Bible passage that didn't specifically mention Jesus, he said that he would 'go over hedge and ditch' to get back onto the London Road to make sure that he talked about Jesus.

It's my conviction that when we tell stories about Jesus, we're always on the 'London Road' and always on the right track. When we talk about him, we help people to see that it's ultimately what we believe about him that really matters – because so many times in our conversations with our friends, we can easily get side-tracked into all of life's little cul-de-sacs. Creation, the Crusades and why God allows suffering are valid topics to explore – but in answering them, my advice is this: always try and make for the London Road as soon as you can. Avoid cul-de-sacs, friends. Go as fast as you can to a Gospel and find a story about Christ.

As we tell a story about Jesus, and keep our focus on him, we cannot help ourselves from sharing what he's like, how his influence impacts upon us and is radically transforming who we are and how he is constantly showing his love and kindness. People can ask us questions for all kinds of reasons. Occasionally it's a smokescreen or a diversion, but more often than not, it's coming out of an honest desire to wrestle with the truth or arrive at some sort of answer to a nagging question. Now there's definitely a place for apologetics, but for most of us in our everyday lives, I have found that the simplicity of responding to these questions from friends with an answer from the Bible is often all we need and is what we see in the Bible itself. It has the power to change lives, and it enables us to focus the conversation on Jesus.

Sharing the Bible, naturally and informally, deepens our relationship with others and allows us to sow the seeds of God's Word in their lives. Let me encourage you, get to know Bible stories, especially in the Gospels. Read them regularly, immerse yourself in them, retell them to others. When you are asked tough questions by your friends, you'll be all the better equipped and empowered to make much of Jesus in your reply.

Friends, whatever else we do, let's tell our friends how amazing Christ is, how much he means to us and what he's like. How handy it is that the Gospels are brimming over with stories about him. Why… it's almost as if they were written for that very purpose!

## THINK IT THROUGH

- Which stories of Jesus immediately resonate with you? Could you memorise them so that you might tell them at an appropriate moment in a conversation?
- Think of someone you've chatted to recently. What Bible story could you have introduced into the conversation? Who will you be seeing in the coming weeks? Ask the Lord to be with you as you talk to them.

4

# THE POWER OF QUESTIONS

Have you noticed that Jesus asks a lot of questions in the Gospels? 'What do you want me to do for you?' he asks the blind man. To the disciples who are quarrelling about who is the greatest, he says, 'What were you arguing about on the road?' To the disciples in the middle of the storm, he says, 'Why are you so afraid? Do you still have no faith?' 'Why do you call me good?' he asks the rich young man who wants to know how to inherit eternal life. To the disciples, 'Who do you say I am?'[15] Questions make us think. They show interest. They help clarify. They build relationship.

A little while ago, I was driving through the countryside with a friend from university who I hadn't seen for many, many years. He asked me how life was going for me – as you do. I told him about my cancer diagnosis and my treatment.

He was shocked. 'That's awful. I'm so sorry. How do you cope?'

I said, 'It's rough, but I find that knowing Jesus Christ helps so much. He's a real friend.'

He was intrigued. 'Really? Do you? That's interesting.'

I replied, 'Yes, I really do. Like this morning I was reading such and such a Bible passage. What about you? Do you have any particular beliefs you rely on?'

He said that he wasn't sure.

But after a moment, he continued the conversation. 'Do you believe hell is a real place?'

We had a long conversation. He was particularly struck by the fact that hell is a place where God is not. If we have chosen to withdraw from God, he gives us that choice and withdraws from us totally. When he does that, we are in a place without all the good things that we normally enjoy, like love, happiness and beauty. It's not hard to imagine that a place like that would be hell.

My friend then poured out questions, prompted I'm sure by the Holy Spirit, and I had the opportunity to ask him a few questions myself, like, 'What puts you off the Christian faith?'

The great thing about questions is that they allow respectful, generous sharing of the gospel and genuine, interesting conversation. We're not forcing the gospel down someone's throat. We are asking them what they think and really listening to their reply. There is nothing offensive or pushy about that. We will soon realise if they aren't keen to continue the conversation. In that case, we change the subject and talk about something else. That's fine. God is the one who changes hearts, not us.

My all-time favourite question is this: 'I find my faith so helpful. How about you? Do you have any particular beliefs?' I doubt anyone could be offended by such a friendly question. We just need to keep it very simple, low key and non-threatening and allow lots of opportunities for our friends to change the subject if they want to.

I try to take it very slowly and gently. If we've had a good discussion and my friend seems to be interested, I might then ask, 'Have you ever read the Bible?' or 'Did you ever look at the Bible?' Most people haven't, they have no idea of the Bible's content whatsoever. Maybe I'll ask, 'Do you ever pray?'

And if my friend is showing real interest, I will go onto a third question: 'Would you like to have a chat about the Bible with me sometime?' At which point, most people will decline – but *some* will say OK. If we've been telling our friend the story about Jesus in the storm, for example, and they've shown a real interest, it's not difficult to ask, 'If you liked that story, there's loads more. Would you like to have a look at some of them with me?' If someone says 'yes' to this, I will suggest meeting for a coffee and then I use a resource called *The Word One to One* (in a book, app or online) to help me chat through John's Gospel in a natural and easy way.[16]

If you don't think you could ask someone if they have any particular beliefs, how about, 'What do you find your identity and your value in?' That might open up a conversation with a friend about finding meaning in relationships or academic achievement or trying to be a good person. And that might lead on to a discussion about how those things inevitably fail us. If they're interested, we might get the chance to explain how we find that Jesus is so much more fulfilling than relationships or success and about the wonderful freedom of knowing that you're forgiven by God.

If you find asking questions hard, then you may find that the simple act of looking at a Bible passage with a friend one-to-one will inevitably prompt them to ask questions. Any Bible passage does this. Let me give you an example. A few years ago, some kind friends from my university days formed a WhatsApp group so that we could all keep in touch. I posted some psalms that I enjoyed (just a few verses, sowing a few little seeds) and I commented on God's compassion. People questioned it. *Is God really compassionate when he sends people to hell?* So, I went straightaway to Jesus and posted the story of the widow of Nain from Luke 7 where Jesus shows beautiful compassion to a grieving mother. Again, it was a little, tiny seed – a very short story and only a handful of verses. One person then said, 'If you or I had been there and could heal people, wouldn't we have done the same?' In other words, wasn't Jesus just being as compassionate as anyone else would have been? 'Fair enough question,' I said. 'Look at this passage.' And then I posted the story of the thief on the cross. Another seed: again, very short. 'Here,' I said, 'is super-human compassion. As Jesus dies in agony, he thinks of others.'

I hope you get the point. Sowing seed by sharing the Bible in simple, easy-to-understand portions is bound to prompt questions in a really natural way.

## A HUGE LEAP

Christians sometimes say to me that it's a huge leap from 'How are you? I haven't seen you for twenty years' to talking about the gospel. Or maybe we're thinking about someone we see several times a week and how difficult it would be to talk to them about Jesus. We chat happily about this and that – but somehow never get onto very important issues.

I try to talk about things that matter and ask how people really are, rather than spending all the time asking about someone's job or where they're going on holiday. Or maybe I'll just say, 'I'm so enjoying church at the moment' and see if they pick up on it. If a friend tells us a problem, we might ask, 'Would you mind if I prayed for you?' I also try to ask people questions that I would like to be asked. For example, 'How about you? Do you think there is anything after death?' If we get to know people and have proper conversations, I guarantee some opportunity will arise. And pray that it does!

It's very important that we see friendship as a wonderful gift, whether or not our friends choose to follow Jesus. We must never see it as a means to an end, but as a gift – second only to friendship with God himself. Our friends must know that we genuinely love and appreciate them for who they are and that we treasure the gift of our friendship with them.

## HEARD IT ALL BEFORE

For many of us, the hardest people to talk to about the gospel – and keep it on the agenda – are close family members or friends who've heard it all before. We worry about damaging a relationship that we're in for a lifetime. This is hard. We want to be respectful and un-intense, while recognising that the issues at stake are eternal, not just for our lifetimes.

You'll need to work out for yourself what is appropriate for you to say to your loved ones. But let me tell you about my beloved older cousin who is an atheist and who has heard my arguments for believing in God many times. In fact, he could probably present them much better than I can! If I'm chatting to him and feel I want to sow some gospel seed, I ask him politely, 'Do you mind if I say something…?' Or 'Tell me if I'm going on about this too much.' Or 'Stop me if you don't want to talk about this.' Poke fun at yourself and don't take yourself too seriously. It's important that we check in with people about how much they want to talk about God. If they don't want to, we must respect that. And if that's the case, then prayer is always the default – and belief in the power of the seed of God's Word. A tiny seed can penetrate the very hardest ground. We'll come back to the power of prayer and the power of God's Word later in the book.

Of course, one of the reasons that we have so few conversations about Jesus might be that we don't really chat much to people who aren't Christians. An over-busy life, including a busy church calendar, is often the greatest enemy of personal evangelism. We may spend so much time learning about 'discipleship' within our Christian groupings, that we are kept far away from the world. Some people have succumbed to the curse of the Christian bubble – all their friends are Christians and their main place to socialise is church. If that's you, it's not too late to do something about it – but it will take time and intention to change our patterns. We will need to think about what we can do and where we can go to have more contact with people who aren't Christians – and we will probably also have to think about what we'll need to give up to create space in our week.

## THE BEAUTY OF QUESTIONS

The great thing about asking questions is that it is respectful and unthreatening. We listen to how our friend responds. Are they interested? Do they ask us further questions? Or do they shut down the conversation rather awkwardly? Either is fine. We just react accordingly – by talking some more about Jesus, or by shutting up and changing the subject! We leave God to be the one who moves people's hearts. We listen and we engage with people where they genuinely are.

Questions – and checking if our friends mind if we keep on about Jesus – also stops us from going too fast.

We should be like a footbridge to Jesus that people can go over and meet him when they're ready. By far the most common mistake is to try and drive an enormous juggernaut across that is too heavy for the bridge. For example, if someone doesn't even think Jesus was a real person (which is apparently true of around 40% of the UK population), we shouldn't launch into a discussion on the atonement or expect them to sit through a 40-minute sermon.[17] We need to be patient and take our cue from our friend. Are they interested or not? Let them set the pace. Questions are great for that.

Sometimes people think that getting their friend to church or an event is the key thing. However, invitations like that can come much too early and they also risk destroying the bridge. This is especially true in a context where people are exhausted from work and may live miles away from church or from the event that we'd like to ask them to. Events are convenient for Christians, but not necessarily for our friends. Instead, I'd suggest a coffee and a quick look at the Bible together. Or just a coffee and let them ask you anything they like about the Christian faith.

For churches, I suggest that a double-barrelled approach to evangelism is needed. In the past, it was all 'come and hear' not 'go and tell'. In the initiative 'A Passion for Life', which I co-chair, we aim to equip Christians to go and tell others, as well as inviting friends to church events.[18] We need both. Questions, by the way, are vital in church events and modern technology allows this to be done very easily. Visitors can post questions (anonymously, if they want). People can vote on which questions they'd like to be answered. All in all, it's a great way for discussions to be tailored to the questions of the people who are there.

## MY FAVOURITE QUESTIONS

I was asked the other day what my favourite questions are. Which are the ones that lead to the best conversations and don't make my friend feel uncomfortable? I've mentioned my all-time favourite already: 'I find my faith so helpful. What about you? Do you have any beliefs you rely on?' The reply isn't usually very thought out or articulate, but you very soon get a sense of whether your friend wants to continue the conversation or not – and that's helpful. It's not remotely pushy and you can back off right away if you sense they don't want to talk.

I also like asking, 'What puts you off the Christian faith? I'd be really interested to know.' You're immediately flagging up that you want your friend to be honest with you and it can open up a good conversation. Often they will relay a bad experience they had in a church – often, sadly, that people were unfriendly. Or they may bring up some of the recent scandals. In reply I would say, 'Oh, I'm sorry to hear that' and make it clear I'm not here to defend the church.

If someone has shared with me about an awful situation they're in, I sometimes ask, 'Can I pray for you?' If they say yes, I ask, 'What would you like me to pray for?' Or I might say, 'Would you mind if I read you a psalm?'

I usually choose Psalm 23 because if there is one passage in the Bible that people might know, it's this one. And it's dead easy to say a few wonderful things about the Lord, if it's appropriate.

From Psalm 23, I would show someone that God is personal and that he is a shepherd, taking care of his flock. He promises to be with us when we walk through the valley of the shadow of death. I can also tell them that that's been my personal experience. The Lord Jesus knows the path through the valley of the shadow of death and, through his resurrection, he has defeated death itself. God doesn't promise us a bypass around the valley, but he promises something much better – his presence in it. And, because of him, I know where I am going – the house of the Lord. Home. Keep it simple and apply the passage to yourself. Centre it on Christ.

I recently had a big birthday party with many, many guests and God so arranged it that one of my friends ended up sitting next to a Buddhist friend of mine on her left and a Hindu friend of mine on her right. The next day, completely independently, both my friends said to me, 'I really loved talking to Katie. She was so warm and friendly. She told the story of how she came to faith and how God has helped her with her daughter's life-threatening illness since then.' This warmth had made an immediate impression on them – far more than the best marshalled argument.

Author and evangelist Becky Pippert also thinks questions can be powerful in talking to people about Jesus.

She describes an occasion where she got chatting to a lady called Sue who was sitting next to her on a plane.

> *I had work that I had planned to do, but since she was quite chatty and seemed to want to talk, I put away my materials and silently asked God to guide our conversation.*
>
> *I began by asking questions to learn who she was and to see where we might have common interests. It didn't take long before we discovered that we both liked to travel and learn about different cultures, and that we both loved books, jazz, and films.*
>
> *Then Sue began sharing some of her views, and I quickly realized that we had very different worldviews. (This, of course, is where we often stumble as Christians, because we aren't sure what to say when someone makes a statement we do not agree with.)*
>
> *At one point in our conversation Sue said, 'I really believe in the essential goodness of human nature.'*
>
> *I asked her, 'I'm just curious – what do you think about the state of the world? How do you think society is doing?'*
>
> *'Oh, the world is falling apart. It's a mess!'*
>
> *'Ok, so help me understand how the world can be a mess when it's filled with entirely good people!'*
>
> *'That's a very good question!' Sue said. Then she offered [her] analysis.*[19]

Becky says that she always looks for common ground to connect. She's careful to respect them and their views and agree where she can. She'll always start with silent prayer

– and sometimes she'll have the opportunity to ask, 'Can I tell you my story? It's a long one!'

Questions can be gentle and respectful. They give us an opportunity to listen, to get to know people, to be a real friend. Sometimes they give us the opportunity to speak of how Christ has helped us and what he means to us.

## THINK IT THROUGH

- I talk here about my favourite questions. What questions might work best with your own friends and family members in chatting about what they believe?
- Think of the person you find it the hardest to share the gospel with. Can you imagine using this question-based approach with them? What might you ask?

# 5

# THE POWER OF WEAKNESS

I've been living with incurable cancer since 2015, and I've lost count of all the different medical problems and treatments that I've experienced. But I've found, very strangely, that this suffering has given me so many opportunities to tell others about hope in the face of death. You can read my story in my books, *Beyond the Big C* and *Hope in the Face of Suffering*, but you'll find that the books are not really about me. My story is just a little, rather insignificant garden path up to a wonderful house where I found hope that lives not just for a moment, but for all eternity. That house, of course, is Christ.

Isn't it curious that my suffering has made people willing to listen to me? God used the suffering of Christ to redeem the world, and he can use our suffering, infinitely smaller though it is, to point others to himself. Our weakness and suffering make us vulnerable, and that vulnerability can be unthreatening and attractive. People often think that Christians are arrogantly looking down on them and that we have everything together, but our suffering corrects that misunderstanding. It's as if God uses it as a small ramp onto the bridge that opens the way home to God.

Some of us will be going through a rough time at the moment, others will not. Whatever our circumstances, I would venture to say that there has never been such a good time to be a Christian in the UK than now. Life is uncertain and there are many challenges. Of course, we must never be opportunistic or blasé about what we and others are going through – we should be loving and gentle with our friends. The fragility of life is something we should approach with reverence, respect and humility. But, if we are kind and sensitive, I think that we have an amazing opportunity to talk about the hope which is ours in the Lord Jesus Christ. And our own weaknesses and struggles, in particular, bring us extraordinary opportunities to speak about Christ.

## HOPE IN TIMES OF TROUBLE

When somebody dies – whether it's someone we know very well, or a disaster we read about in the news – it brings us face-to-face with our own mortality. In Jesus' day, a tower collapsed and eighteen people died. Jesus was questioned about the event and his full reply is in Luke 13. One of the things Jesus said was that disasters are a big wake-up call. When something awful happens or someone dies, we think about the world differently. C S Lewis said that pain is '[God's] megaphone to rouse a deaf world.'[20] When the news is full of wars and disasters, it makes us think about our own death and the incredible uncertainties of life. When disaster strikes, the hamster wheel of daily life suddenly stops turning.

Uncertainty presents a unique opportunity to speak naturally about our hope in the midst of challenging times. We have an enduring hope – and, during weakness and suffering, we have an incredible opportunity to talk about it. This is an area where we will hopefully feel extremely comfortable and at home. There will be spiritual topics and questions that we find hard to answer. However, when it comes to the hope that burns within us, we will often find that we have plenty to say.

## CONVERSATIONS ABOUT CHRIST

We can start the conversation simply and gently. Here's a typical imaginary conversation. For example, 'Jeremy, how can you be so cheerful or optimistic?' Having had cancer for nearly ten years, I have lots of conversations like this. They just seem to land in my lap through the Holy Spirit. People often ask me, 'How do you keep going?' I might say something like, 'Well, I definitely couldn't have gone through it without Christ.' Maybe the conversation ends there. That's fine, it is not our responsibility to force a conversation. God is the ultimate evangelist and the Holy Spirit will guide us.

But maybe the conversation goes on, and I might ask my friend, 'How about you? How do you try to make sense of what happens when things go wrong?' Or 'How about you, do you have any particular beliefs?' Or 'How about you, do you think there is life after death?'

By simply asking questions, soon enough in my experience, you will sense if there's a chance for you to speak. Or perhaps your friend may ask you a question and then you can be honest in your reply.

Another approach is to say something like, 'I find it so helpful being a Christian because I find Jesus – or my faith – gives me hope.' Now, you may wish (and indeed really want) to expand on that – but let the other person direct the conversation so your friend never feels under pressure. When they stop talking about the gospel, you stop talking. If I can put it like this, you can suggest a direction of travel, but allow them to steer the boat.

## HOPE IN HOPELESSNESS

One of the reasons that difficult times are such an opportunity to share about Jesus is because he gives us hope when the situation is hopeless. We must tread with great compassion, following in the footsteps of the Lord. I've already spoken about the grieving widow of Nain in Luke 7. There's a real poignancy in Jesus' reaction: 'When the Lord saw her, his heart went out to her and he said, "Don't cry."'

Let's be like the Lord – full of kindness and compassion. Let the suffering person guide you as to what they want, rather than trying to seize control of the situation. As my wife points out, I'm always trying to fix things. Incurable cancer is sadly, by definition, unfixable. So, what does compassion look like? With a fellow cancer sufferer, I'd go straight to a psalm and read a few verses and explain how they have helped me.

The key thing is to be with our suffering friends and to listen to them. Listen, empathise and try to understand their feelings rather than judge them. Look, for example, how Jesus deals with Martha. Grieve with the grieving. See how the Lord wept at the tomb of Lazarus.[21]

If the suffering person invites you onto their 'boat' of suffering, don't try and 'seize the tiller' once you're on board. After you've listened to them, listen some more. Wait until you sense they want something from you. Once you sense that it's appropriate – then and only then – ask them gentle questions.

For example, 'Would you mind if I prayed for you?' Or 'Would you mind if I read you a psalm?' When you pray, please be honest about how they feel. Use their words and offer them up to God. You are helping the person speak to God about what they are going through. It's always important to be honest with God in prayer. After all, he knows exactly what we're feeling.

## HOPE IN THE PSALMS

This experience is, of course, just like the psalms. I absolutely love going to the psalms with suffering people in suffering times. I sometimes start with the psalms even before I turn to the Gospels. The psalms are so helpful because they contain every possible human emotion –

grief, doubt, despair, loneliness, anger, feeling troubled – I could go on. What I would suggest is simply reading one of the shorter psalms, and then make a couple of comments about how you found that helpful.

Let's take Psalm 23 as an example again. You could say many, many things about this wonderful psalm. Ask the Holy Spirit to direct you at that time to find the right words. But here are a couple of very simple things you could say about it.

'The Lord is my Shepherd.' I find this so helpful because I believe there's a personal God whom I can know, who cares for me. He is *my* God, and I am his son or daughter, or his sheep, if you prefer.

'Even though I walk through the darkest valley [or through the valley of the shadow of death, in the older versions], I will fear no evil, for you are with me.' This verse speaks to me so wonderfully because I find, as I walk through the valley of fear, I'm not alone; God is indeed with me. In the hospital, strapped to the gurney with my head in a claustrophobic mask, he is there.

Or we could say, 'I'm afraid of death, but I know God, and he helps me, he comforts me.' We might say: 'Jesus is Emmanuel – meaning "God with us" and I've found that to be true.' My central theme is that I always, always, always try to talk about Christ. And I try to use easy-to-access words, not churchy, intense theological words. Good theology is vital, but it must be communicated in easy-to-understand ways.

It is key to explain any technical terms. 'Sin' is a good example. What does that mean? Lots of people don't know. I love Aleksandr Solzhenitsyn's quote, 'the line dividing good and evil cuts through the heart of every human being.'[22] There are no truly evil people or truly good people. Some people may be very evil or very good – but the truth is that *all* have sinned and fallen short of God's glory.

I try to talk about Jesus in the same way that I'd talk about football or my work. 'I find that Jesus is such a friend. I love to read stories about him – like the one I was reading today about when he and his followers were caught in a storm…' Listen to yourself next time you're talking about church. Did it feel as natural as saying you're looking forward to watching the FA cup or that you're really enjoying your current project at work?

## A PRECIOUS HOPE

Do you feel weak? If we have experienced weakness and suffering ourselves, we have a unique opportunity to talk about the hope we have in our Saviour. When we are weak, he is strong.[23]

When we are walking alongside others who are suffering or troubled, we can pray for an opportunity to talk to them about the precious hope we have and introduce them to Christ. Jesus was a man of sorrows and acquainted with grief.[24] Christ suffered.[25] He understands. Friends, this is amazing. We don't have a remote, impersonal God. We have a God who, because he became human, experienced human suffering – suffering far beyond anything we will ever know. Generally, we have no choice about whether we suffer or not. But he willingly and voluntarily suffered because of the love that he has for us, to bring us back to God.

However faltering and nervous we are, we can do no greater kindness to our friends who are laden down with suffering than to take them to the suffering God-man, who can and will help them, and who can and will help us.

## THINK IT THROUGH

- Suffering is never easy and many who suffer testify to the presence of real friends as a source of great support. How can we serve those who suffer?[26]
- How can we bring the comfort of the Psalms or other passages of Scripture into the lives of our suffering friends or family?

6

# THE POWER OF ENTHUSIASM

I love Watford FC and, given the chance, I will be there at Vicarage Road cheering them on. My sisters aren't big football fans, but they'll come along to keep me company. Or if you don't like football, then think of a great restaurant you've been to recently or a fantastic box set you've enjoyed. It is just so natural to enthuse about those kinds of things to other people. Being enthusiastic about something comes easily when you have experienced something good. Take the restaurant. 'That place is amazing,' you say, 'Superb food. The main course was delicious. The setting was stunning and it was excellent value for money. I'm definitely going back.'

## LACKING IN ENTHUSIASM?

Somehow, when we're talking about Christ, we can often sound less than enthusiastic. Why is that? Let me suggest two reasons.

The first is that it's easy to be a bit tepid when it comes to Christ. A bit like a mug of lukewarm tea. We don't experience enough of him – and I certainly include myself here – and so we don't talk about him with enthusiasm. He is like an 'OK' restaurant which we are very familiar with, but which isn't much better than any other restaurant. It's fine – but don't go out of your way to go there. We can sometimes feel a bit half-hearted about Jesus, if we're honest. (As the church in Laodicea in Revelation 3 found out, that is a dangerous position to be in.)[27] We don't talk about him much because we don't feel much. No one enthuses about a so-so restaurant or the disappointing box set.

But there is another thing.[28] If you go on about a fabulous restaurant or a box set, nobody is going to mind. Even if you recommend a Japanese restaurant and your friend replies, 'Oh I really don't like sushi,' no offence is taken. But in our highly pluralistic society, to recommend Christ is to risk causing offence. And most of us don't like doing that.

The answer, of course, is to go deeper into Christ, to know him more, to love him more. To taste and see that he is good. Then we will have something we want to talk about. And don't worry about getting carried away – we can always check in with the person we're talking to and check we are not offending them. 'Would you mind if I told you about…?' or 'Please tell me if I offend you by going on too much about Jesus.'

## TWO SIDES OF THE SAME COIN

We tend to put 'evangelism' and 'how we live' into two separate boxes, but the Bible sees them as closely connected. Peter's first letter shows this very clearly: the well-known command to be ready to give an answer for the hope we have is in the middle of a lengthy encouragement to live godly lives.[29] In one breath, Paul urges the Christians to live radically distinctive lives. In the next, he asks them for prayer that he would have an open door for evangelism.[30] There's no distance between godly living and evangelism. They're intertwined. They're two sides of the same coin.

I fear we are sometimes drawn into thinking that if we are to be effective evangelistically, we need to be more like the world. We think that people won't listen to us if they think we're weird or different. But Paul would tell us to stand out and be different. We *need* to do that. We shouldn't be frightened of not being the same as everyone else (not that we should become unnecessarily weird or objectionable, of course).

When looking at the Christians in the early church in his book, *Evangelism in the Early Church*, Michael Green talks about:

> *...the quality of their lives. Their love, their joy, their changed habits ... Their community life, though far from perfect ... was nevertheless sufficiently different and impressive to attract notice, to invite curiosity ... in an age that was as pleasure-conscious, as materialistic and as devoid of serious purpose as our own. Paganism saw in early Christianity a quality of living ... which could not be found elsewhere.*[31]

Christians *should* look and feel radically different. But in practice, we are often not that different from our non-Christian friends. And, on top of that, we are also *afraid* of being seen as different. Either of these things would be enough to stop us sharing our faith – but when both of them are true, they are super-effective at silencing us.

The Bible sees discipleship and evangelism as two halves of the same whole. One reason that many of us find evangelism so difficult is that we haven't really made progress in our discipleship. Just being told to 'tell others about Jesus' is difficult if we are not living for Jesus, loving Jesus, following him as we should and delighting in him. The stronger our discipleship and the deeper our love for Christ, the more naturally we will talk about him.

I suggest we need to do as the apostle Peter does and address both issues – evangelism and discipleship – together. We will only grow in one aspect if we grow in the other. Right now, I fear we live in a bit of a *vicious circle* where our lack of distinctiveness means we don't talk about our faith and our silence means our discipleship never blossoms. What I suggest we need to do is, with God's help, create a *virtuous circle* instead: little by little, our lives become more distinctive and, at the same time, we start to be much more willing to talk about our faith. We find that as we talk about Jesus, we delight in him more and more and long to be like him.

In a way, it doesn't matter where you start on the 'heads and tails' side of the coin – whether it's with evangelism or discipleship. I say this because one danger with evangelism is that we give up before we get started, because we are very aware of our weak discipleship. But evangelism, even if done in a faltering way, will help our discipleship because it is an essential part of the expression of our faith. In short, we see that the power is not in us but in the Word. My experience is that the more we do evangelism, the more natural and more fun it becomes. Our faith grows. We think, 'Actually, I can do this, however weakly and feebly. And I am enjoying seeing God at work.'

God honours even our feeble baby steps of obedience to his Word and the stronger the right leg becomes as we totter forward on shaky legs, the stronger the left one will become as it follows it. Galatians 5 tells us that we need to keep in step with the Spirit. Let's keep in step with him on two legs – evangelism and discipleship. The more we are in Christ, the bigger the difference he will make to our lives. The more we are changed by the Holy Spirit, the more we will want to share him with others.

## WE'RE IN IT TOGETHER

It's also worth noting when thinking about the relationship between discipleship and evangelism that Jesus' final instructions to his disciples were a *collective* call to make disciples.

At the end of Matthew's Gospel, in what's known as the Great Commission, Jesus said:

> *When they saw him, they worshipped him; but some doubted. Then Jesus came to them and said, 'All authority in heaven and on earth has been given to me. Therefore go and make disciples of all nations, baptising them in the name of the Father and of the Son and of the Holy Spirit, and teaching them to obey everything I have commanded you. And surely I am with you always, to the very end of the age' (Matthew 28:17–20).*

Did you notice the word 'doubted'? Even after the disciples had spent time face-to-face with the risen Lord, some of his closest followers still doubted him. Isn't that surprising? The Bible is a realistic book. Some of the disciples doubted and were fearful. Jesus neither criticised them for this, nor told them to go and get their issues resolved before they could carry out the task of making disciples. He simply told them to go – and then he left them. He was able to do this because all authority has been given to him.

J I Packer said, 'Evangelism is man's work, but the giving of faith is God's.'[32] We can go and make disciples because God promises us that, through his church, he will call those who are his children to follow him and they will become his disciples. We can't do anything on our own – but he can do everything. And that's exactly what has happened in the two thousand years since: starting with a tiny handful of followers, millions and millions have been added.

It is easy to be individualistic when we are thinking about evangelism. We in the West are quick to think about things in terms of what it means to us individually – but if we look at what happened next (in the book of Acts), it is the church *together* making disciples, not individuals battling alone. We are not all called to be ministers baptising or teachers teaching – but we are all called to simply tell others about Jesus Christ. In Acts, we see that the explosive growth of the church came through all the different parts of the body of Christ pulling together to make disciples.

And notice the emphasis on making 'disciples', not converts. We are called to a lifelong service of Christ. In nineteenth-century America, the church became obsessed with 'making a decision for Christ' at large evangelistic rallies. People like Charles Finney and others emphasised the decision rather than discipleship. It's not about a one-off, dramatic, individual response. It's about living together in an everyday manner as part of Jesus' church with a changed heart posture and a changed life through meeting Jesus Christ.

Maybe you still lack confidence. Many of us do! I absolutely include myself. Many of us feel like Moses in Exodus 3 and 4 when God told him to go to speak to Pharaoh and rescue the Israelites. Moses wasn't sure about this... What if they don't believe me? But I don't know what to say. I'm not very eloquent. Can't you send someone else? (I'm sure we all ask those questions from time to time.) God refused to let Moses off the hook – but he promised to help him: 'Now go; I will help you speak and will teach you what to say' (Exodus 4:12).

And we must never forget, friends, the crucial last part of Jesus' instructions at the end of Matthew's Gospel: 'And surely I am with you always'. We go to make disciples not on our own, but with the Lord Jesus alongside us. Through his Holy Spirit, he will be with us and help us and give us the right words to say. Through the power of his Word, he can change lives. And when that happens once or twice, our faith grows and we realise that his mighty promises are just as true today as they were two thousand years ago.

## THINK IT THROUGH

- How enthusiastic do you feel about Jesus Christ and the gospel?
- Do you think there's anything that's holding your discipleship back?

7

# THE POWER OF SOCIAL MEDIA

Christians are often afraid of social media and technology – but I find it one of the easiest platforms on which to share my faith. In fact, I'd call it a ministry. Not everyone has this ministry. Some people regard social media as unhelpful – and, of course, that can be a risk. Overall, though, I wish there were more Christians who were active and saw technology as an opportunity rather than a threat. Whether it's Facebook, Instagram, TikTok or BeReal – or wherever you spend your time – there are real opportunities for the gospel in the way that we use social media.

When the printing press was invented, one of the results was the spread of God's Word. Now we have another huge technological leap forward. Let's make sure that we make use of the fantastic reach it offers to share his Word.

## WISDOM FROM PROVERBS

Of course, we need to be wise in the way we use social media and the way in which we communicate.[33] The things that make social media so valuable are also what can make it so full of temptation – we must guard our hearts! Proverbs has some good general wisdom which can help us think about how we use social media.

> *Above all else, guard your heart, for everything you do flows from it. Keep your mouth free of perversity; keep corrupt talk far from your lips (Proverbs 4:23–24).*

> *Fools find no pleasure in understanding but delight in airing their own opinions (Proverbs 18:2).*

> *To answer before listening – that is folly and shame (Proverbs 18:13).*

> *Fear of man will prove to be a snare, but whoever trusts in the Lord is kept safe (Proverbs 29:25).*

So, we must guard our hearts. The internet is full of temptations and if they are a particular problem for you, it's good to acknowledge that and settle on other ways of sharing the gospel that work better in your situation.

## LISTENING AND SHARING

But for me, social media is great! In my opinion, it is best viewed not as a preaching platform but a way of sharing our lives, faith and all. We need to *listen* as much as we share, if not more.

It can be tough expressing certain views on social media – as it is in the real world. As Rico Tice says, we have to be willing to cross that pain line and express unpopular opinions. The key question for us is: are we more afraid of our friends' opinions of us, or of God's?

My experience with social media has been very positive. My cancer helps tremendously – I know that is a strange thing to say! My experience with cancer treatment gives me something which I hope is interesting to communicate, and provides a springboard for sharing my faith.

Recently, for example, I posted a picture alongside this verse:

> *Then come, let us go up to Bethel, where I will build an altar to God, who answered me in the day of my distress and who has been with me wherever I have gone (Genesis 35:3).*

And I wrote this:

> *Jacob's proposal below is mine too. I'm feeling OK, I'm glad to say, after my gruelling radiotherapy which finished ten days ago. Some side effects but mild compared*

*with the previous radiotherapy when at the equivalent time in recovery I was in hospital. I will soon find out if it worked: your prayers if you are a praying type should be, please, that the tumours in my brain would have gone or been greatly reduced. I feel God answered my prayer for strength and his presence has always been with me. Unlike Jacob, I've no need to build an altar though as I have Jesus with me whatever happens. Even through death itself. He makes all the difference.*

Forgive me for 'tooting my own horn', as our American friends say. This is fairly typical of my posts. I nearly always include one Bible verse because the supernatural, transformative power is not in anything I write but in God's Word. But I always try and apply it to myself, briefly explain what it means and, crucially, make it personal. There is a risk here, of course, that I become the story rather than Christ. But our lives and our experiences, if handled well, can point people to Christ. If we want a biblical pattern, look at Paul. He often tells the story of his road to Damascus experience, but the 'hero' of his story is Christ, not himself.

In the same vein, I also tweet a Bible verse every day and make a short comment, often explaining why the verse is helpful to me. As always, I believe our central focus should be sowing God's Word. My story works well on social media, which is about opening up our lives.

Of course, this means we also need to engage with our friends' lives and stories, genuinely caring about them, and about their views and experiences. Social media is not just about our posts but how we engage with others. It's speaking the language of those we want to reach.[34] Seeing who 'likes' our posts might also show us that one of our friends is more interested in gospel content than perhaps we'd realised.

## ENCOURAGEMENT

Christians in the days of the early church lived in a society that was antagonistic and they met to encourage each other. I've really appreciated the mutual support and encouragement I've received through social media. It's so easy to get discouraged. A friend of mine, Le Fras Strydom, set up a 'Bible Sharers' group on Facebook to enable us to encourage one another.[35] Recently a lady in the UK shared how she had been looking at Bible passages with a couple of friends on Zoom. Her friends had both had some contact with Christianity in the past but felt they knew very little. She said how thrilled she was by the fact that they were so interested in looking at the Bible together and by all their questions and desire to know more. We were all encouraged by the fact that she told us about it!

The more we can encourage each other and share questions and challenges and ask each other for prayer (as I'm sure the early church did, albeit not on social media!), the more we will see things happening and be encouraged to try ourselves.

## THE INTERNET AND CHURCHES

Being open to using technology applies to churches as well as to individuals. It's easy to focus on the negatives of technology – worrying, for example, that streaming church services online will result in Christians staying home, watching on the sofa and not coming to church. This fear about threats and ignoring opportunities is very short sighted. Imagine we were in management in the Premier League. Imagine we said to the general public that they could only access our football games if they came and watched them at the stadium. No TV or radio or highlights. If we owned a Hollywood studio and said, 'No availability on Netflix or Amazon Prime. You must always come to the cinema.' We don't have to settle for in-person-or-nothing ways anymore. Using today's technology, there is now no reason why we can't offer a hybrid model by which people can access our services – and especially evangelistic services – either in person or via the internet. In retrospect, especially for evangelistic orientated events, isn't it staggering that we weren't doing this already?!

Today, people like to consume information on their own terms and at a time that suits them. When I have done evangelistic events, I have found that once they are uploaded onto the web (and especially when the video is shared online by the people who attended the events), they typically get five to ten times the number of views than the original number who attended. This also means we have to think about how to promote such content. One of the best routes is to get church people to share talks they attended and liked on their social media channels. Organisations like 'Speak Life' produce very clever, short videos – you can share those too.[36] When you do, explain why you liked it. Make your witness personal and engaging.

## THE INTERNET AND THE YOUNG

We should also mobilise our youngsters. In my experience, they thoroughly enjoy the opportunities that social media and the internet have opened up. Evangelical churches can be highly risk averse. We seem to be worried about everything. Sometimes I think we have adopted Queen Victoria's saying by accident, 'Change? Why would we want to change? Things are quite bad enough already!'

If we are going to reach young people, we need to let them experiment and be creative. I'm not suggesting in any way that we depart from the core truths of the gospel – only that the *means* of communicating it must change. Rather than big evangelistic church events, after which we tend to collapse, it often works better for churches to organise regular, small events. Bottom-up is good. Creative is good. Unleash those creative energies in your church, particularly among the young.

People talk about how we're living in an 'attention economy' with various platforms desperate to keep you on their app or looking at their content. We have precious opportunities in life and on social media to speak into the noise and gently direct people's attention towards Jesus Christ.

## SHARING OUR LIVES IN PERSON

Of course, one of the dangers of social media is that people can hide behind their mobiles and computer screens. It's all too easy for someone to post something that they'd never say in person. But being a Christian is about a real relationship with our God, and real, in-person relationships with other people.

The Christians in the days of the early church have got a thing or two to teach us about this. No social media, obviously – but they lived in exceptionally challenging circumstances. They faced daily persecution and possible death because of what they believed. Let's take a little detour to think about how and where they did their evangelism. As we read through the New Testament, especially in Acts 17–21, we'll see that people's houses were very significant – for example, Jason's at Thessalonica, Titius Justus' in Corinth, Philip's house in Caesarea, and many others.[37] We see their homes being used for prayer meetings, evenings of Christian fellowship, communion, a whole night of prayer, impromptu evangelistic gatherings, and times of formal teaching and answering questions.

Today, most of our evangelistic efforts occur in church. This made sense in the past when church attendance was much more common for most people, but it makes much less sense now when few non-Christians will be in our buildings – and it is often daunting for them to come (and also for us to ask them). Church meetings and services certainly did happen in the early church, but they tended to be for Christians. In fact, deacons would often guard the door to keep non-Christians out and at a certain point in the service, those seeking to become Christians but not yet admitted (*catechumens*) would be asked to leave.

Surely we must go out in the way that the early church did and use a wide variety of methods, both online and in person, to spread the good news of the Lord Jesus. I fear we have become somewhat unimaginative since Constantine made Christianity the official religion of the Roman empire and we expect people to come to us. But the biblical command is not only to invite them to come to us but, in particular, for us to go out. Sometimes the best ideas are the simplest ones. Having people over for a meal and getting a Christian friend to come and share their story. Or running a bookstall in the local high street, maybe? A friend of mine did a murder mystery over a meal in their house with a short talk from me afterwards on 'The greatest mystery of all time – did Jesus really rise from the dead?' We can try something – and if it doesn't work, try something else. As we meet people in informal and accessible settings, the Word of God will do its work and they will get used to hearing what is in the Bible. Then, when they hopefully and eventually come to church, they will understand what it's all about.

We need to be much more patient in walking our friends along the path towards faith. This includes allowing them to ask questions, argue and debate with us. None of this means we should stop preaching evangelistically in church – in fact, every sermon should have something of the gospel, but we cannot anymore rely on this as the only way of making disciples. We need to be biblically flexible on *how* we communicate while being consistent on *what* we communicate.

## THINK IT THROUGH

- Would it work for you to use social media more? Before you post on social media, pause, pray and ask God, 'What are the wise gospel words for me to use right now?'
- What creative ideas might there be among members of your church? What creative ideas do you have yourself?
- Might you be able to use your home more for sharing your life and the gospel with your friends and colleagues?

8

# THE POWER OF PRAYER AND THE HOLY SPIRIT

My friend John MacKinnon is always reminding people about the importance of prayer in evangelism. He has an interesting perspective on prayer and says:

> *Prayer is work. Prayer is hard work, and it needs to be the engine room of church life. If truth be told, we would rather make plans than pray.*[38]

Is that true of you? Many of us find it difficult to pray regularly and consistently for our friends to come to know Jesus. John is from Scotland – a nation that has rich history of times of revival where God 'moved in incredibly significant ways, waking up His church, mobilising His people, and calling sinners to Himself in extraordinary ways.' John goes on to point out that one of the greatest lessons we learn from those remarkable times is that people prayed. People prayed and prayed – and God worked mightily.

In the book of Acts, we see remarkable growth in the church. That little band of disciples didn't keep what they'd discovered about Jesus to themselves. As we've said, Jesus had told them to 'go and make disciples of all nations, baptising them in the name of the Father and of the Son and of the Holy Spirit, and teaching them to obey everything I have commanded you.'[39] He'd also given them a wonderful promise, 'you will receive power when the Holy Spirit comes on you; and you will be my witnesses in Jerusalem, and in all Judea and Samaria, and to the ends of the earth' (Acts 1:8). He knew that this bunch of all-too-human, flawed people wouldn't be able to take the message of repentance and faith to Jerusalem, then to Judea and Samaria, and then to the rest of the world. They just weren't up to it. But God was. The disciples were promised that the Holy Spirit would empower them in their evangelism. That same promise of the Holy Spirit's enabling is for us too.

## I CAN'T DO THIS – BUT GOD CAN

None of us can share the gospel and point people to Christ without the help of the Holy Spirit. Without him, we are totally weak – that's why depending on him is utterly essential. The evangelism prayer we all need is, 'Oh Lord,

I just can't do this, I'm afraid, please help me.' In one sense, it's very simple. We need to pray. Pray before we talk to our friends, pray while we're talking to them about Jesus – and pray afterwards as well!

Evangelist John Chapman used to pray every day, 'Lord, please give me an opportunity to speak for you today, and please don't be subtle with me!' He knew he found it easy not to scatter a little gospel seed, even when there was an opportunity right in front of his nose.

Why is it that we spend so little time in prayer for our friends? Why don't we ask God for specific opportunities to speak even simply about Christ? Perhaps we forget that we can do nothing without him. Realising and admitting we can't do it or that we are afraid or that we find it difficult is a good place to start. If we ask God, he will send us his Holy Spirit to help us in our helplessness.

Richard Borgonon says:

> *I have learned to pray that my friends are convicted of their need for Christ. How? By their being convicted of their sin and realising that, without his forgiveness paid for them through his cross, their sin remains with them. If we have this firmly rooted in our prayers then we shouldn't be surprised that Christ will answer such a prayer with a breakthrough that we just couldn't have imagined.*

## THE EARLY CHURCH AND THEIR USE OF THE BIBLE AND PRAYER

Those early Christians knew how vital prayer was, as evangelist Michael Green tells us:

> *To the use of the Scriptures the early Christians added prayer as a prime necessity in all evangelistic enterprise. When the Twelve poured out their hearts in prayer they were filled with the Holy Spirit, they spoke the Word of God with boldness, and multitudes believed.*[40]

Prayer was absolutely key:

> *It was … with the Scriptures and prayer as their main weapons, backed up with love, their burning zeal to share their faith with others and the sheer quality of their living and dying that the early Christians set out to evangelize the world.*[41]

## QUIET PLACES AND CORPORATE SPACES

I have found John MacKinnon's idea of 'quiet places and corporate spaces' really helpful.[42] He quotes the Scottish preacher David McIntyre who said that the only things we need are a quiet place, a quiet heart and a quiet hour. I wonder where your favourite quiet place is. Is it a particular chair, a place where you love to walk or maybe the bathroom where you can lock the door. We need a quiet place – somewhere we can be still before God and pray.

A quiet heart comes from bringing ourselves intentionally into God's presence as we start to pray. The opening prayer on the Lectio 365 prayer app models this focused attention on the Lord: 'I pause to be still; to breathe slowly, to re-centre my scattered senses upon the presence of God.'[43]

And the quiet hour may not be sixty minutes precisely – but it's time carved out of the busyness of life when we prioritise speaking to the Lord. Some people like to use a journal to jot down what they are learning about God and keep a note of people they're praying for. Others prefer apps like PrayerMate.[44] Some people use prayer cards or a simple piece of paper. It doesn't matter. We're all different. The important thing is that we pray!

Quiet places. And corporate spaces. We've already talked about the early Christians in Acts. We read how 'They all joined together constantly in prayer' and that 'they devoted themselves ... to prayer'.[45] Notice those words – constantly, devoted. Praying with others is often so encouraging. We can say 'Amen' to their prayers and lift our hearts and minds and friends to the Lord. The task of taking the gospel to all nations becomes a shared one, not a burden that we're trying to carry on our own. And it's a shared joy when friends respond to God's invitation.

## OPEN A DOOR

I wonder if you know of anyone who prayed for you before you knew the Lord. I'm eternally grateful to my parents who prayed for me. It's very common – in fact,

I would say that it's usually the case – that when someone turns to Christ, they later discover that someone (or a number of people) had been praying for them quietly in the background. Praying that the Lord would open the door of their heart to his message of salvation.

As Paul says to the Colossians:

> *And pray for us, too, that God may open a door for our message, so that we may proclaim the mystery of Christ, for which I am in chains. Pray that I may proclaim it clearly, as I should (Colossians 4:3–4).*

We're not in chains – but we do need to ask the Lord to open a door for us so that we can speak about him. And when he does, we ask him to help us to proclaim it clearly – even if we are saying something very small and simple.

## THE WORK OF THE HOLY SPIRIT

Each and every one of us must be born again – even the most religious of us. Nicodemus, in John 3, was the epitome of what it looked like to be religious. He was a member of the Jewish ruling council and a Pharisee. He even believed that Jesus had come from God because of all the miracles he did.

Jesus' words to this religious man are striking: 'Very truly I tell you, no one can see the kingdom of God unless they are born again' (John 3:3). Nicodemus was incredulous. *How can anyone be born again?* he asks. *It's impossible!* And he was absolutely right, of course. No one can go back into their mother's womb. It's unimaginable.

But Jesus insists. 'You must be born again,' he tells him. The language the Bible uses is so stark. Jesus speaks in these terms because the difference between someone who has put their trust in Jesus and someone who hasn't is as radical as the difference between someone who is alive and someone who is dead. A person without Jesus is like someone who has died. They are 'dead' in their sins, as Ephesians 2:1 puts it. Blind. Simply unable to see the truth of the gospel. What's more, the devil actively tries to block the truth. 'The god of this age has blinded the minds of unbelievers, so that they *cannot see* the light of the gospel that displays the glory of Christ' (2 Corinthians 4:4, my italics).

Sometimes we find it hard to accept that this is true of our unbelieving friends and family. After all, they are often so lovely, so much kinder and more generous than we are. Can it really be true that they are actually dead in their sins? That's what Jesus is telling us. Trusting in him is not about being slightly nicer than we were before. It is a radical transformation. It is about being born again. And only prayer and the work of the Holy Spirit can give people that new birth and a totally transformed life.

We easily get bogged down and feel we are making little progress and seeing few results. But all we have to do is ask. Oh, how difficult this is – I know from my own experience. We struggle on in our own strength – but we must ask for *his* strength. And we must be persistent. Jesus told a story about a widow who went to a judge, pleading for justice (Luke 18). The woman wouldn't give up – she just went on and on at him, a bit like a mosquito buzzing round and round all night. In the end, the judge (who happened to be unkind and ungodly) gave in and did what she asked – just to get rid of her! Jesus tells this story to encourage us. If a wicked judge ended up helping this woman because she kept asking, how much more will our loving Father help us. We need to take encouragement from this and keep going in prayer for our loved ones.

I was reading a book called *Burning Steel* by Peter Hart recently – letters, diaries and eyewitness accounts about a British tank regiment trying to advance in Normandy in the Second World War.[46] The German anti-tank positions held the high ground as they were well camouflaged and dug in and they simply picked off each British tank as it rolled forward. One after another the tanks were blown up. There was an awful choice – a dreadful scramble to bail out of a burning vehicle, or the terrible consequences of staying inside it. Bravely and obediently each tank rolled forward to obliteration.

Fortunately, the Allies had total command of the air and, after a period of bitter losses, the commanders figured out how to call for support. They'd ask for what they code-named 'Lime Juice' – rocket-firing Typhoon aircraft which blasted the German defences and opened up a path to advance. We don't need aircraft power – but we do need Holy Spirit power. Without him, we can do nothing. But with the intervention of prayer, all things become possible and the devil's grip is loosened. People are born again only by the work of God – not by us. But we are his agents. We can spread the word and he uses that to transform people and enable them to be born again. The ultimate evangelist is God, not us. He uses us, for sure – but we must ask for his help. In countless ways throughout Scripture, we are reminded that with Christ, nothing is impossible.

## THINK IT THROUGH

- Why don't you create a prayer list of family, friends, neighbours or colleagues that you long to come to know Jesus, for whom you could pray regularly?
- Here is a simple prayer that God will give you the opportunity to speak about him today, 'Lord, lead me to the people that you are drawing to yourself.'

9

# THE POWER OF GOD'S WORD

How are you feeling at this point? Encouraged? 'I think I might be able to do this... I might be able to ask a question and get a conversation going. I like the idea that it's up to God whether the seed takes root or not, that it's not down to me. That's rather liberating.' Or are you feeling sceptical? 'Great in theory, but I can't see this working for me...'

## THAT'S NOT OUR JOB

Can I just remind you of something? You will never convert a single person in the whole of your life. That's not your job – it's God's. You will never need to pressurise someone into becoming a Christian. Giving new life is the work of the Holy Spirit. In fact, you don't even need to know all the answers – you've got Christian brothers and sisters you can ask. Above all, you've got a resource – the Word of God that comes pre-loaded with the Holy Spirit. Just be a page turner and a Bible sharer – and pray.

You've got a church you can invite people to, books you can read to inform yourself, or books you can give to someone who's asking questions you can't answer. Our job is simply to scatter seeds. Scatter a few seeds, pray and let the Word do its work.

An example of this from the Bible is Philip and the Ethiopian man he met on the desert road (Acts 8). God gives Philip an 'open goal'. He can hardly miss! And what leads to the open goal? The power of God's Word. An angel tells Philip where to go and soon he comes across a man reading from the book of Isaiah. Philip asks him if he understands what he's reading. '"How can I," he said, "unless someone explains it to me?" So, he invited Philip to come up and sit with him' (Acts 8:31).

I always wonder how the Ethiopian eunuch got the scroll. Somebody presumably told him about Jehovah and his written Word. Won't it be amazing in heaven if someone comes up to us and tells us how a conversation we had with them, or a social media post we shared, helped them on the path to Christ? But I'm going off track… Philip shows us exactly what we need to do. 'Do you understand what you're reading?' he says. It's a perfect model in how to look at a Bible passage with someone else! That's all we need to ask. Do you understand what you're reading?

Friends, I believe with all my heart that if we sow seed, we will see results – either in this life or the life to come.

Why? Because God's Word is tremendously powerful. One of my sisters gave a teenage boyfriend a Bible and was amazed to find, more than thirty years on, that he still had it and read it. Seed grows.

Converting people is not our job. Our job is to sow seed and give people an opportunity to know that there is a God and that we can know him through his Son Jesus Christ. How can we know him? Through reading an account of his life in one of the Gospels.

## SMALL IS BEAUTIFUL

Even small amounts of God's Word can work miracles. My friend Richard Borgonòn brought someone to faith through sharing John's Gospel and *The Word One to One*. Sometime afterwards, the new Christian said to him, 'You had me at the first words of John's Gospel. When I heard the words, "In the beginning," I suddenly thought to myself, "I've been a fool. Dawkins is wrong. There has to have been a beginning." And when you read, "...was the Word," that led me to the person in the beginning.' All he'd read was the first phrase of the first verse of the first chapter of John's Gospel, 'In the beginning was the Word...' Six words. That was all he needed!

We are talking about scattering seeds, remember? We don't need to give everyone everything in the first conversation. Or, to change the metaphor, if we send too much heavy traffic across the bridge, it might collapse. We don't need a full Bible overview or everything there is to say about a tricky question. Just a verse. Maybe even just a phrase. In John 4, Jesus says that 'One sows and another reaps'. We don't have to do everything. We may just sow a seed and never see how it grows. That may be someone else's privilege.

Seed is small but it grows unseen because of its intrinsic power.

## KNOW YOUR BIBLE

How well do you know your Bible – and especially the Gospels? This isn't a guilt trip – it's just that if we don't know the Bible stories very well, we won't be able to share them. I'm not talking about quoting Bible verses at people – but knowing it so well and being so immersed in it that you can drop it into any conversation, almost without realising. The more natural and seamless and less 'clunky' we can make our Bible use the better. One lady described it to me as 'speaking naturally about Jesus from the Scriptures'. I love that.

My friend Paul Eddy had a good idea. He bought some cheap index cards and, when he was reading God's Word, if a verse jumped out at him, he would write it on a card – a yellow card for promises and a green one for action. He kept the card with him during the day which meant he kept thinking about it and could learn it off by heart. As the cards piled up, he started to build a collection of God's promises to dwell on and a reservoir of relevant texts on different topics. We could do the same with stories or passages that might be particularly good to share.

Do we really believe what it says in our Bibles? Do we really believe that those without Christ will suffer 'eternal and irreparable loss'?[47] The early disciples did. That is why they were prepared to go to their deaths rather than renounce Christ. They believed that there was a real heaven and a real hell – and that the people around them needed to know. The early disciples passionately believed that Jesus was the way, the truth and the life and that no one could know God without him. If we don't really believe that Jesus is unique, we will never cross the pain line of telling our friends. If all roads lead to God anyway, what's the point? Those early disciples thought it was a matter of life and death. Do we?

Strangely, it is a good thing that many people know little of the Bible because it presents us with a huge opportunity. There is supernatural power in God's Word. The Bible can look daunting to our non-Christian friends. It's a big book and it's not designed to be read as most books are – from beginning to end. As we grow in our knowledge of God's Word, we will be increasingly happy to talk about it with our friends.

Some of our friends will know quite a lot. Maybe they're from a Christian home or even studied Theology. But maybe they'd also like to read a passage of the Bible and chat about it with us, all the same. We won't know unless we ask. We might be surprised by their reaction.

## THE WORD

Looking at one of the Gospels with a friend is a great place to start and *The Word One to One* or *Uncover* booklets are amazingly easy to use and entirely geared to being user-friendly to your non-Christian friend.[48] In my experience, people find the Gospel story – and especially Jesus as a person – so powerful and so fascinating, particularly if they don't know much about him. Someone told me recently that 25% of people thought Harry Potter was in the Bible. If that's even remotely true, it means we need to make sure we explain basic terms such as 'Old and New Testament', 'grace' and 'sin'. We will want to avoid using confusing cross references. We will need to explain that you don't just read the Bible cover to cover, like you do with most books. The Ethiopian man I mentioned earlier said to Philip, 'I need someone to explain this to me.' Can we be that 'someone' for one of our friends?

## WHERE IS THE POWER?

Dear Reader, if you have read all this and maybe still don't think you could be so active in sharing your faith in relaxed conversation, can I just point out that the power really is in the Word and not in you? Please don't tell me you could never be a Bible sharer because all the evidence is that Christ and the Holy Spirit will be at work as you simply turn the pages of the Gospel with your friend, and just answer their questions.

The Lord works through his Word and great is the joyful blessing for the Christian as they get to see him at work!

## PUT YOURSELF IN THEIR SHOES

If we get to the point where we can invite a friend to church or an event, we must try and put ourselves in their shoes. We often organise things for our own benefit at a time and place that suits us. I can assure you that's not how the world works. When I was starting out in private banking, if I'd asked a prospect (a wealthy person) to come and see me at my office at a time that suited me I'd have been given short shrift. If I wanted someone to do business with me, I'd always put myself out to arrange things to suit them.

Non-Christians understandably often feel very nervous about coming to a church building because it's an alien experience. We might feel the same if a friend invited us to a mosque, or a betting shop! We should find accessible times and places to meet which suit them and not us. This is not to say that we should give up inviting people to church or to guest services but that our first thought should be to present them with invites which are accessible, appealing and convenient – not just somewhere where *we* feel comfortable! This, it seems, is also highly biblical. Yes, the apostles sometimes taught in synagogues but if we look at the book of Acts, it was mostly wherever people could be gathered. In the marketplace, out on the streets, wherever people were.

When inviting a friend, we must be very clear about the Christian content. There is nothing worse than people feeling taken aback or deceived once they discover what they're coming to. And even if our invite is clear as to the purpose of the event, we shouldn't inflict things which will make them uncomfortable. Loads of singing might be one obvious example!

We must realise, friends, that we are in a spiritual battle. Nobody can move someone else one inch nearer to Christ by their own efforts. To be born again we need a miracle, the supernatural intervention of God in our lives. We can start by realising that we can't do it, but God can – and he chooses to use us, his weak and sinful ambassadors, to pass on the good news about Jesus Christ.

## HOW

So how are we going to go about scattering gospel seeds? We're bound to feel a bit nervous. But we don't need to be a theological expert and we don't need to know our Bibles backwards. Here are a few top tips I've picked up along the way.

Make it clear what you're asking and don't set the bar too high. Something like, 'Do you want to have a coffee sometime and I can show you another passage like the one we talked about?' If we say something like 'Do you want to read the Bible with me?', they may think we mean the whole Bible and be thoroughly put off! Once you've had that coffee, if it goes well, see if they want to do it again or not. A one-off is fine too. Just a tiny bit of God's Word may have a huge impact on them.

Encourage them to ask questions – not just on the Bible verses. Anything that occurs to them. Discussion is good.

Don't worry if someone gives you a flat 'no'. That's fine. Talk about something else. From experience, I reckon that about one in four will say 'yes' to a trusted friend making this kind of suggestion. That means that three will probably say 'no'. We can keep praying for them.

For your encouragement, the *Talking Jesus 2022* report showed that one in three people want to know more about Jesus after having a conversation with a Christian friend about their faith. And 24% of people who come to follow Jesus do so through reading the Bible.[49] It's worth putting up with 'no thank you' a few times to find the ones who are curious, or maybe even hungry to discover God's love for themselves.

## THINK IT THROUGH

- Think of four people you could ask to look at a bit of the Bible with you. Some of them will probably say 'no', but maybe one of them will say 'yes'!
- Try to think of the best way to ask them. Why not start praying for them right now and aim to pray for them every day?

10

# THE MIRACLE OF SALVATION

In one of the letters that Paul wrote to the church at Corinth, there's a section that's just perfect for us to look at as we think about this task of scattering gospel seeds – or perhaps we should call it a privilege rather than a task. Here it is:

> 1 *Therefore, since through God's mercy we have this*
> *ministry, we do not lose heart.* 2 *Rather, we have renounced*
> *secret and shameful ways; we do not use deception, nor do*
> *we distort the word of God. On the contrary, by setting*
> *forth the truth plainly we commend ourselves to everyone's*
> *conscience in the sight of God.* 3 *And even if our gospel is*
> *veiled, it is veiled to those who are perishing.* 4 *The god of*
> *this age has blinded the minds of unbelievers, so that they*
> *cannot see the light of the gospel that displays the glory*
> *of Christ, who is the image of God.* 5 *For what we preach*

*is not ourselves, but Jesus Christ as Lord, and ourselves as your servants for Jesus' sake.* [6] *For God, who said, 'Let light shine out of darkness,' made his light shine in our hearts to give us the light of the knowledge of God's glory displayed in the face of Christ (2 Corinthians 4:1–6).*

I just want to remind us of three things.

First, do you see in verse 4, that the god of this age has *blinded* the minds of unbelievers? Because of that, they *cannot* see the light of the gospel. It's the gospel that displays the glory of Christ and because they are blind to that, they are blind to God himself. That's the reality of it.

Second thing: We preach Jesus Christ as Lord – see verse 5. We don't preach ourselves. That would be no use. We're no better than anyone else and we certainly can't save anyone. Not 'preach' as in sermons, of course – 'preach' as in tell other people about Jesus. Sowing seeds of gospel hope.

And thirdly, verse 6, God makes his light shine in our hearts. He's the one who does the work of bringing light so that the blind people can see. What a relief. It's his work, not ours. He is the one who is responsible for the miracle of salvation. And it is a miracle. From darkness to light. From death to life.

## GO FOR IT!

So, let's get on with it, shall we? God has made each of us different, we all have a different story and different friends and family. What works for me might not work for you.

The important thing to remember is that it's the Lord who shines his light and draws people to himself, he is the one who performs the miracle of new birth – not us.

Ask for wisdom and the Holy Spirit will guide you. Being fearful is natural. I'm fearful too! What I find helps me overcome my fear is taking that first step forward.

Last week, I received the most encouraging email.

*Dear Jeremy,*

*I wanted to share with you about _________. You spoke with him at the end of your talk when you came to our church. He'd heard about the event from friends of his in our church, so he travelled down (hundreds of miles). Not long before the event, he had received a diagnosis for cancer.*

*Your conversation with him was hugely helpful. Subsequent to that he found a church local to him, and over the following few weeks and months became a Christian. His cancer was terminal, and he died a few weeks ago and is now with his Lord and Saviour in glory. I wanted to let you know as an encouragement for you, but also to say thank you for your ministry over the last few years.*

Friends, God is at work! The Holy Spirit prompted a sick man to drive hundreds of miles to hear God's Word. Let's go out and seek the lost, confident in the power of the Holy Spirit and the Word of God. The fact that that man drove hundreds of miles shows how God prompts the lost to seek him. We must just scatter the seed – and God will be at work silently and supernaturally.

May Almighty God help you and bless you as you take the first step, as I do, conscious of fear but relying on him to help you. May he encourage you as you aim to scatter tiny little seeds of hope in your conversations with friends and loved ones, in the knowledge that the power lies with him, our sovereign Lord, and in his Word.

# MY STORY AND YOUR STORY

One of the easiest stories to tell is your own story. How did you come to Christ? What was it about Jesus that captured you? What truths about the gospel struck you first? Which truths didn't dawn on you until later? What is it that you love about Jesus right now? How is he helping you day to day?

As Michael Green points out, personal testimony was a keynote in the early church – by all the people, not just the leaders of the church.[50] They were all enthusiastic about what Christ had done for them. They didn't impose themselves on others or make themselves objectionable – but they didn't back off from telling other people about their own experience either.

It's possible to overdo testimony, of course, and make ourselves and not Christ the focus of the story. But I believe that introducing the main topic, Christ, and talking about our own experience of him can be both biblical and effective. Our culture will often be willing to listen to our experience when it will reject our objective truth claims.

Telling someone our experience is like the first gear in a car: it gets the journey moving. As quickly as possible – and as smoothly as possible – we want to move into the highest gear which is talking about Christ.

Let me tell you how I use my story when I'm chatting with friends. It can go something like this:

Friend: Lovely to see you, Jeremy. How are you doing?

Me: It's been so tough. (Tell latest story of gruesome treatment!)

Friend: You are amazing!

Me: Thank you, you are so kind – but actually it's not me, it's Jesus. I find his presence so valuable. I couldn't keep going through all this mess without him. How about you, do you have any particular beliefs? (Show genuine interest in their answer, ask questions, show love and care for your friend.)

Me: Did you ever look at the Bible?

Friend: No! (Usual answer)

Me: Would you like to sometime? I've got lots of friends who do. We simply sit down over a coffee and look at one of the eyewitness accounts of Jesus' life and the explanatory notes and I try and answer their questions. I'd love to do that with you. What do you think?

Sometimes people ask me how I became a Christian in the first place. Then I'll say something like this: I was brought up in a very Christian home and I hated it, especially church. Like all of us, I was a rebel by nature. Then two things happened. First, every summer, we went Bible smuggling behind the Iron Curtain and I was struck by the belief of these Christians who had every reason not to follow Christ, yet showed a tremendous joy in doing that in the teeth of persecution. Secondly, one day, as I was listening to someone reading the Bible, it all clicked. I knew that Jesus was a real person and that I could know him here and now. I felt my heart 'strangely warmed' and I realised that the Bible was true and that I could know Jesus myself.

When I finish telling a friend my story, I usually say something like, 'What about you? Do you have any particular beliefs you rely on?' and we continue to chat.

## REMEMBER, REMEMBER

That's my story, but what's your story…? What first convinced you of the truth of the gospel? Can you remember? It's easy to forget and it's easy to lose our 'first love' for Christ.[51] God was always telling the Israelites to remember what he'd done for them – because they so easily forgot. Peter tells us in his letter that we need to be ready to give 'a reason for the hope you have'.[52]

Can you explain what you love about Jesus Christ? Is it at the forefront of your mind?

Take some time to think through these questions and write down your answers so that they are fresh in your mind next time you're chatting with friends and loved ones.

**What was the first truth about Jesus that thrilled your heart?**

**How did you come to faith in Jesus? Was it over a period of time, or were you suddenly captivated by his love?**

**What aspect of Jesus' character do you love most? Can you explain why?**

**Which bits of the Bible have spoken to you recently? How?**

**What truths has God been teaching you recently?**

**What prayers has God answered recently?**

**Which is your favourite Bible story? Why? Can you explain its message and why you love it in a couple of minutes?**

**Which is your go-to passage when things are tough? In what ways does it encourage and strengthen you?**

**How would you answer the question, 'Who is Jesus and why does he matter?'**

**Prayerfully consider – what is holding you back from sharing your faith in Jesus more often?**

Don't gloss over these questions. Answering them will take time but it will be worth it. You'll know what you want to say when an opportunity comes up. Could you take one question a day and give it some thought? Make sure that Christ is always the focus when you are talking about your own story of faith. Now pray for an opportunity to share it clearly and succinctly when the opportunity arises.

If you take the time to do this, you will genuinely be able to say, 'The other day, I was remembering when I first started thinking about Christianity...'

# OVER TO YOU

The next page is for you to write down what you're going to try out. Are you going to try asking a work colleague over a coffee or a pint, 'How about you? Do you have beliefs you rely on?' Or can you think of a question that might work better for you? Maybe 'What do you find your identity and your value in?'

Or are you going to pray for an opportunity to talk about the Bible story that you've been thinking about? Perhaps you'll note down how you could explain your journey with Christ to a friend. Look back over the different chapters of this book and think what the Lord is laying on your heart. Have you concluded that you're not spending enough time with non-Christians to be a real friend to them? Has prayer been too low on your agenda? Over to you and the Lord…

# RESOURCES

## THE WORD ONE TO ONE

I'm always going on about *The Word One to One*. It's the best way I've found of talking about the Bible easily and naturally and in a bit more depth, if someone is prepared to do that with us. Have a look (https://www.theword121.com).

## UNCOVER

*Uncover* is another resource that lots of people love. There are three versions to help you and a friend explore one of the Gospels (Mark, John or Luke). It works in a similar way to *The Word One to One* – some questions and short bits of explanation (https://www.uncover.org.uk).

## A PASSION FOR LIFE

On the 'A Passion for Life' website (https://www.apassionforlife.org.uk/train-in-evangelism/), you will find resources and videos that aim to encourage, equip and enable Christians to share their love for Jesus. There's input on answering tough questions and why prayer is so important, for example.

## TELLING STORIES

Maybe you feel you're not very good at telling stories. How about reading a children's Bible for a good paraphrase? Maybe something like *The Jesus Storybook Bible* by Sally Lloyd-Jones.[53] Or a translation of the Bible that is in everyday English, like The Good News Version, the New Living Translation or The Message which are all freely available online (https://www.biblegateway.com).

For those of us who like technology, you could try an artificial intelligence chatbot like ChatGPT![54] Put something like this into the search box: 'Retell the Bible story of the stilling of the storm from Luke 8:23–25 in a creative way.' See what comes out! Technology is extraordinary.

I've also written another book called *Meeting Jesus* which answers some common big questions using Bible stories in everyday language. It has been designed to give away to a non-Christian friend – but it will also help encourage you and give you some ideas about how to retell Bible stories.

But the best thing is to practise. Give it a go and see what the Lord does.

## HOW TO EXPLAIN THE GOSPEL

It's not often that people directly ask us what the Christian message is. But if they do, we want to be ready! If you're not sure you know how to explain the gospel, have a look at the Christianity Explored website (https://www.christianityexplored.org).[55]

Or try an incredibly simple outline along these lines:

- God created everything – it was all good. But human beings chose evil.
- God did something about evil by becoming a human 2,000 years ago in the person of Jesus and we can know about his life, death and resurrection from the eyewitness accounts in the Gospels.
- Christians believe that Jesus is God, that he died for our sins, that he came back from the dead – and they follow him. What do you think about that?

In talking about sin, the Fall, judgement, etc., I would avoid using words like 'man' (to mean all people) as that can put many people's backs up, and 'fallen' won't mean much to most people. I'd also avoid the word 'sin' and say something like 'we chose evil' instead. I think that pointing to the Gospels is absolutely essential as it makes the key point that Jesus was a real person and encourages our friends to read one of the Gospels with us – and that's where the power lies, not with us.

## PRAYER

PrayerMate is a fantastic app that helps Christians get more organised about praying regularly for people and causes they care about. Available here: https://www.prayermate.net/app.

# ENDNOTES

1 Savanta ComRes, *Talking Jesus Report 2022*, https://talkingjesus.org/wp-content/uploads/2023/08/Talking-Jesus-Report-A4-AUG-23-WEB.pdf.

2 Acts 9.

3 Rico Tice with Carl Laferton, *Honest Evangelism* (Good Book Company, 2015), p. 17.

4 Matthew 19:13–14; Luke 9:51–55; e.g. Luke 8:23–25, 9:13; Matthew 26:56; John 4:31–35; Mark 9:34.

5 James Montgomery Boice, *Acts: An Expositional Commentary* (Baker Books, 1997).

6 See, for example, John 4.

7 Jonathan L Griffiths, *Preaching in the New Testament* (IVP Academic, 2017), p. 46.

8 Michael Green, *Evangelism in the Early Church* (revised edition, William B Eerdmans, 2004), p. 380.

9 Luke 15:11–32.

10 Mark 4:33. I acknowledge, of course, that the parables were also designed to some extent to hide truth – but, in the main, Jesus taught the crowd with stories and with illustrations.

11 Luke 15:11–32, Luke 24:13–35, John 11:17–37, Mark 4:35–41, Luke 22:39–46.

12 Hebrews 4:12.

13 Luke 24:27.

14 C H Spurgeon, *The Soul Winner*. Quoted in blogpost: https://www.thegospelcoalition.org/blogs/justin-taylor/spurgeon-on-preaching-christ/.

15 Mark 10:51, Mark 9:33, Mark 4:40, Mark 10:18, Mark 8:29.

16 *The Word One to One*, https://www.theword121.com.

17 'Jesus "not a real person" many believe', BBC News, 31 October 2015.

18 I've been overwhelmed by the positive feedback about the training from 'A Passion for Life', especially from churches that have never really done anything before. Don't know where to start? Start here! https://www.apassionforlife.org.uk/train-in-evangelism/.

19 Rebecca Manley Pippert, *Stay Salt – The World Has Changed: Our Message Must Not* (The Good Book Company, 2020), p. 182.

20 C S Lewis, *The Problem of Pain* (Harper Collins, 1996), p. 91.

21 John 11:1–44.

22 Aleksandr I Solzhenitsyn, *The Gulag Archipelago (1918–1956)*, trans. Thomas P Whitney, vols 1 & 2 (Harper & Row, 1973), p. 168.

23 2 Corinthians 12:10.

24 Isaiah 53:3, ESV.

25 1 Peter 4:1.

26 You might find my book *Hope in the Face of Suffering* helpful. It is a book of Bible passages that I found helpful when faced with suffering and death (10Publishing, 2021).

27 Revelation 3:14–22.

28 These thoughts emerged from a conversation with my friend, Robert Strivens.

29 1 Peter 3:15, in the midst of 2:11–5:11.

30 Ephesians 4:17ff, Ephesians 6:19–20.

31 Green, *Evangelism in the Early Church*, p. 381.

32 J I Packer, *Evangelism and the Sovereignty of God* (InterVarsity Press, 1991), p. 40.

33 Tim Chester's short book, *Will You Be My Facebook Friend?* (10Publishing, 2012), is helpful. One of the things he says is that, 'Facebook does not cause sin, but it can accelerate it because it liberates us from the constraints of the body.' For example, people will say or do things online that they would never say or do in person.

34 Trevin Wax, 'Four Things a Pastor Should Consider Before Engaging Social Media', 3 February 2014, https://www.thegospelcoalition.org/blogs/trevin-wax/4-things-a-pastor-should-consider-before-engaging-social-media/.

35 https://www.facebook.com/groups/biblesharers.

36 https://speaklife.org.uk.

37 Acts 17:1–9, 18:7–11, 21:8ff.

38 John MacKinnon, 'Prayer in Evangelism', A Passion For Life training video, https://www.apassionforlife.org.uk/videos/prayer-in-evangelism/.

39 Matthew 28:19–20.

40 Green, *Evangelism in the Early Church*, p. 202.

41 Green, *Evangelism in the Early Church*, p. 203.

42 MacKinnon, 'Prayer in Evangelism'.

43 Daily prayer from the Lectio 365 app, 24-7 Prayer, https://www.24-7prayer.com/resource/lectio-365/, which aims to help you pray the Bible every day.

44 PrayerMate is a great app for helping us pray regularly. Available at https://www.prayermate.net/app.

45 Acts 1:14, 2:42.

46 Peter Hart, *Burning Steel: A Tank Regiment at War, 1939–45* (Profile Books Ltd, 2022).

47 Green, *Evangelism in the Early Church*, p. 382.

48 *The Word One to One*, https://www.theword121.com. *Uncover*, https://www.uncover.org.uk.

49 Savanta ComRes, *Talking Jesus Report 2022*.

50 Green, *Evangelism in the Early Church*, pp. 316–317.

51 In Revelation 2:4, the risen Christ says to the church in Ephesus, 'Yet I hold this against you: You have forsaken the love you had at first.'

52 1 Peter 3:15–16, 'But in your hearts revere Christ as Lord. Always be prepared to give an answer to everyone who asks you to give the reason for the hope that you have. But do this with gentleness and respect, keeping a clear conscience, so that those who speak maliciously against your good behaviour in Christ may be ashamed of their slander.'

53 Sally Lloyd-Jones, *The Jesus Storybook Bible: Every Story Whispers His Name* (Zondervan, 2007).

54 Chat Generative Pre-trained Transformer, https://chat.openai.com/chat. If you don't like the output, you can tell it to try again and instruct it to retell the story more creatively or ask it to avoid using clichés, for example!

55 https://www.christianityexplored.org/Groups/276316/Home/CE_ORG/What_is_Christianity/What_is_Christianity.aspx.

Beyond the
Big C
Hope in the face of death
Jeremy Marshall
JEREMY MARSHALL
Meeting
JESUS
INTRODUCING THE ANSWER
TO OUR BIGGEST QUESTIONS
HOPE
in the face of
suffering
20 daily devotions
for tough times
Jeremy Marshall